BARCELONA

Knopf MapGuides

P9-AGU-490

Welcome to Barcelona!

This opening fold-out contains a general map of Barcelona to help you visualize the 6 large districts discussed in this guide, and 4 pages of valuable information, handy tips and useful addresses.

Discover Barcelona through 6 districts and 6 maps

A La Barceloneta / El Born / La Ciutat Vella

B El Raval / El Barrí Gótic / La Ribera

C Sarrià / Pedralbes / Sants

D L'Eixample / Gràcia

E Montjuïc / Poble Sec / Sant Antoni

F Port Olímpic / Poblenou / La Dreta del Eixample

For each district there is a double-page of addresses (restaurants – listed in ascending order of price – cafés, bars, tearooms, music venues and stores), followed by a fold-out map for the relevant area with the essential places to see (indicated on the map by a star ★). These places are by no means all that Barcelona has to offer, but to us they are unmissable. The grid-referencing system (**A** B2) makes it easy for you to pinpoint addresses quickly on the map.

Transportation and hotels in Barcelona

The last fold-out consists of a transportation map and 4 pages of practical information that include a selection of hotels.

Thematic index

Lists all the street names, sites and addresses featured in this guide.

DISTRICTS OF BARCELONA

La Boquería (Mercat de Sant Josep) (B C4)
→ *La Rambla, 91*
Tel. 93 318 20 17
The best-known of all the city's markets, and one of Europe's finest. Recently restored, the main hall has retained its Modernist look. Fish and seafood are at the center, fruit and vegetables around the edges and butcher's stalls in the corners. A feast for all the senses.
Mercat de la Concepció (D C6)
→ *Carrer d'Aragó, 313*
In the heart of L'Eixample, this sophisticated market has been improved by recent renovation; it is now calmer and more orderly.
Mercat de Sant Antoni (E D3)
→ *Carrer Comte d'Urgell, 1*
Daily 8am–8.30pm
Less touristy than La Boqueria but then, perhaps, more authentic. Sun morning: book and

music market.
La Barceloneta (A E3)
→ *Plaça de la Font*
The most popular market. Always well stocked with fresh fish and seafood.
Flea market (F C2)
→ *Carrer Dos de Maig, 186*
Tel. 93 246 30 30
Mon, Wed, Fri-Sat 9am–8pm
Huge bric-a-brac market; bargaining with the stall-holders is obligatory.
Bric-a-brac
Plaça de la Catedral (B D4)
→ *Tel. 93 291 61 00*
Thu 10am–10pm
Jewelry, books, crockery...
Plaça S Josep Oriol (B C4)
→ *Tel. 93 291 61 70*
Sat-Sun
Art market.
Plaça Reial (A C1)
→ *Sun 9am–2.30pm*
Stamps, coins, medals.
Brocanters del Port Vell (A B2)
→ *Moll de les Drassanes*
Sat-Sun 11am–9pm
Knickknacks, jewelry, books.

SHOPPING

Opening times
Mon-Sat 10am–8.30pm. Department stores and shopping centers close at 9.30pm. Many shops still close for a lunchtime *siesta* (2–4pm). Some shops close Mon morning.
Sales
Twice a year: 2nd week in Jan–end Feb and July–Aug.
Department stores and shopping centers
El Corte Inglès (**B** C2)
→ *Plaça de Catalunya, 14*
Tel. 93 306 38 00 (Mon-Sat)
The most Spanish of the big department store. Several branches throughout Barcelona.
L'Illa Diagonal (C B3)
→ *Avinguda Diagonal,*
545–557 / Tel. 93 444 00 00
(Mon-Sat)
Huge American-style shopping mall: Marks & Spencer, FNAC (European equivalent of Virgin Megastore), Decathlon

MODERNIST BARCELONA

Passeig de Gràcia (D B6)
Magnificent landmark buildings of Barcelona: Gaudí's Pedrera, 'Block of Discord', and 'House of Spires'.
La Sagrada Familia (D D6)
Gaudí's masterpiece.
Park Güell (D D2)
Extraordinary garden-suburb project.
→ *Info. from Centre del Modernismo, Casa Amatlle, Passeig de Gràcia, 41*
Tel. 93 488 01 39

AVANT-GARDE BARCELONA

The city is bursting with events and exhibitions on all things Catalan, including town-planning and architecture.
L'Aquàrium (A C3)
Le CCCB (B B2)
Le MACBA (B B3)
Centre Commercial El Triangle (B C3)
L'Auditori and the **Teatre Nacional de Catalunya (F** C3)
Le Port Olímpic (F BC6)

MULTICULTURAL BARCELONA

Carrer de la Cera (B A3) and **Plaça Herenni (C** B•
Two areas where gypsy traditions are still kept alive by local inhabitant•
Carrer Hospital (B B4)
Halal butchers, Pakistani grocers and an atmosphere of the East. Mosque at n° 91.
Dojo Nalanda (B E4)
→ *Carrer Montcada, 3:*
Seek peace at a Buddh meditation center.

CABLE CAR

BEACH

FUNICULAR

CITY PROFILE

- 1.8 million inhabitants
- Surface area of 37.8 square miles
- 16 districts
- Capital of Catalonia and Spain's second capital after Madrid
- 24% of Spanish people speak Catalan

THE BEACHES

A few minutes from the center of Barcelona, 2½ miles of beaches easily accessible by public transport.
Playa del Bogatell and La Mar Bella (F D6)
→ **M** *Barceloneta, Ciutadella / Vila Olímpica, Bogatell,* bus 36, 40, 41, 45, 59
Perfectly equipped (showers and endless restaurants). Special park for cyclists, skaters and joggers.
Information
→ *Tel. 93 481 00 53 (info. on the temperature of the air, the water, the strength of the wind, etc.)*

VIEWS OF THE CITY

For great views over the city and the bay area.
Parc d'Atraccions del Tibidabo (north of **D** B1, off map)
→ *Plaça del Tibidabo, 3*
From the funfair you get the most colorful view. On a clear day you can even see Majorca and the Pyrenees.
Torre de Collserola
→ *Carretera de Vallvidrera al Tibidabo*
The most 'high-tech', panoramic viewpoint. 1,837 ft above sea level in a glass elevator.
Castell de Montjuïc (E B5)
Small fortress perched on the top of Montjuïc hill; dizzying views of the city.
Torre Jaume I i Telefèric (A B3)
The most beautiful, panoramic view of the harbor and the city center.
La Pedrera (D B6)
The terrace of Gaudí's

masterpiece: from behind the chimneys is a surreal view over the Modernist rooftops of Eixample.

ALTERNATIVE TRANSPORT

By boat
Golondrinas (A B2)
→ *Plaça Portal de la Pau*
Tel. 93 442 31 06
Scenic ferry trips around the harbor.
By bicycle
There are more than 62 miles of cycle routes, mainly around Eixample, Sant Martí and the old city. A word of caution: city drivers don't make allowances for cyclists.
Un Cotxe Menys (A E1)
→ *Carrer Esparteria, 3*
Tel. 93 268 21 05
Price 12 €/day
'One less car': cycle rental, guided tours in the evening.
al Punt de Trobada (F D5)
→ *Carrer Badajoz, 24*

Tel. 93 225 05 85
Price 15 €/day
Cycle, tandem and children's seat rental.
By cable car
Transbordador Aeri (AC4)
→ *Torre de Sant Sebastià (Barceloneta) to Montjuïc*
Tel. 93 441 48 20 daily
Price 9 € (return ticket)
Dizzying views of the bay. Not for the fainthearted!
Telephèric de Montjuïc (E C4-5)
→ *Avinguda de Miramar / Estació Mirador*
Tel. 93 443 08 59
Takes you to the castle at the top of Montjuïc hill.
By tram
→ *Avinguda del Tibidabo / Plaça del Doctor Andreu* (north of **D** B1, off map)
Tel. 93 318 70 74
Old, blue-painted trams which run along the main avenue, lined with Modernist buildings. At the end is a stunning panorama over the city. Get out of the carriage to

climb even higher.
By funicular
Funicular de Tibidabo (north of **D** B1, off map)
→ *Plaça del Doctor Andreu*
Tel. 93 211 79 42 (Fri-Sun)
Art-deco funicular equally as colorful as the funfair at the top of the hill.
Funicular de Montjuïc (E C4)
→ *Avinguda de Miramar*
Tel. 93 443 08 59
Sat-Sun (daily in summer)
No impressive views, but a practical way of getting to the Fundació Miró.

MARKETS

Covered markets
→ *Mon-Sat 8am–2pm, 4–8pm*
Each district has its own local market. Stalls selling fruit and vegetables, *charcuteria* (cold cooked meats), fish and seafood. Spanish specialties to take away and kiosks serving Catalan dishes for lunch.

Welcome to Barcelona!

ESPLUGUES DE LLOBREGAT

MONASTIR DE PEDRALBES

PG. DE LA BONANOVA

PG.

SARRIÀ

RONDA DE DALT B-20

AVINGUDA DIAGONAL

AUGUSTA

SANT

PALAU DE PEDRALBES

CARRER DE SANTS

GRAN VIA DE CARLES III

AVINGUDA DIAGONAL DE SARRIÀ

AVINGUDA

Plaça de Francesc Macià

TRAVESSERA DE LES CORTS

SANTS

CARRER DE NUMÀNCIA

C. D'ENTENÇA

HOSPITALET DE LLOBREGAT

AV. DE MADRID

ESTACIÓ BARCELONA SANTS

CARRER DE TA. CREU COBERTA

C. DEL COMTE D'URGELL

AV. DE ROMA

C

PARC JOAN MIRÓ

D'ENTENÇA

C. DEL COMTE D'URGELL

CARRER D'ARAGÓ

GRAN VIA DE LES CORTS CATALANES

C. DEL COMTE D'URGELL

GRA

AVINGUDA DEL PARAL·LEL

CARRER

EL

CALLE DE BADAL

MUSEU NAC. D'ART DE CATALUNYA

FUNDACIÓ JOAN MIRÓ

RONDA DEL LITORAL

JARDÍ BOTÀNIC

MONTJUÏC

CASTELL DE MONTJUÏC

RONDA DEL LITORAL

E

A

0   500   1000 meters

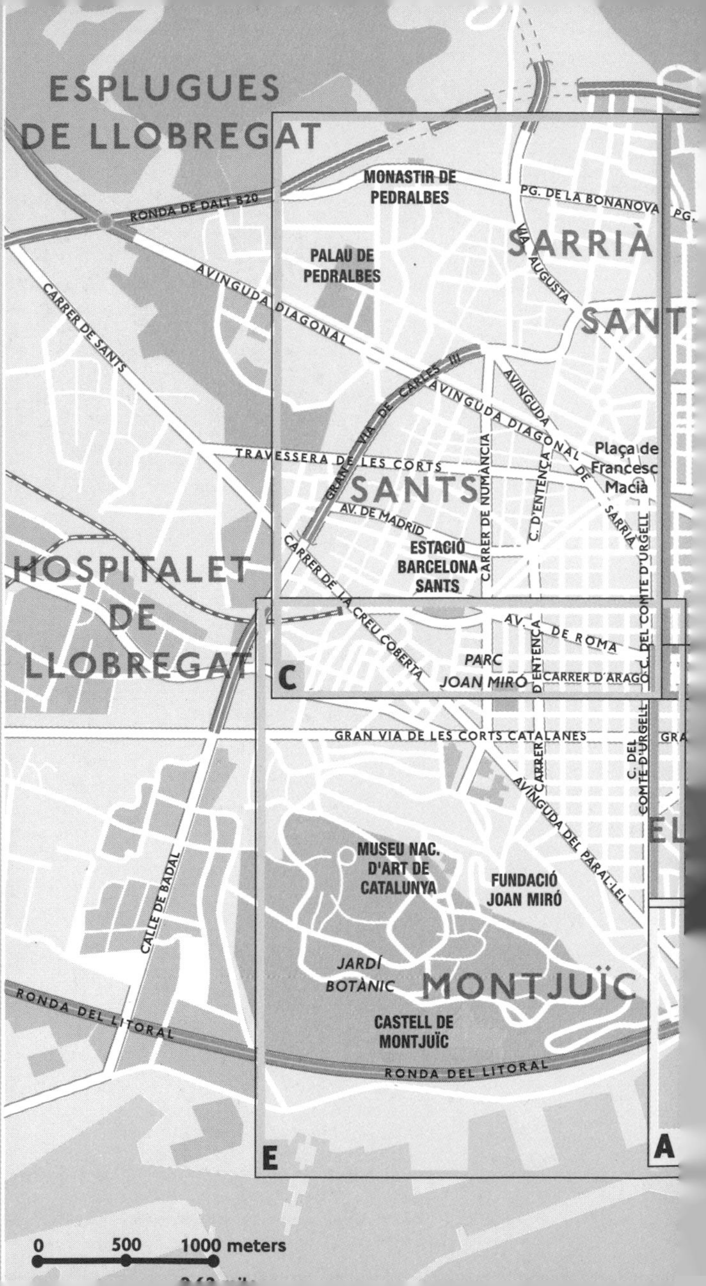

VIEW OF THE TIBIDA

Go BCN
→ *Monthly, free (music shops, trendy shops, bars)* The latest information on what's hip in Barcelona.

MUSEUMS

Opening times
Tue-Sat 10am–7pm; Sun 10am–2pm. Weekly closing on Mon (except Macba which is closed on Tue).

Reduced-price tickets
Concessions are mainly available for over-65s, under-12s and students.

Articket
→ *Available from the participating museums, by phone at Tel.Entrada, or at Caixa Catalunya banks.* Free entry (one visit to each museum) to Mnac, Macba, Fundació Joan Miró, Fundació Antoni Tàpies, CCCB, Centre Cultural Caixa Catalunya. Price 15€.

USEFUL NUMBERS

Police
→ *Tel. 091 or 092*
Fire service
→ *Tel. 080*
Tourist office (**B** C3)
→ *Plaça de Catalunya, 17 Tel. 90 630 1282 (from Spain) 93 368 97 30 (from abroad)*

CALENDAR OF EVENTS

January
Procession of the Three Kings (Epiphany eve, 5th).
February
Carnestoltes (carnival).
April
Festa de Sant Jordi, patron saint of Catalonia (23rd).
Book festival (23rd)
May/June
Comic strip show (May);
Marató de l'espectacle: 48 hours of theater, dance, circus, music, poetry (end May/early June);
Festa de la Diversitat:

three days of multicultural festivities (end May/arly June);
Festa de la Bicicleta (Sun end May/early June);
June
Sónar: international festival of electronic music (three days), has the CCCB (Barcelona Museum of Contemporary Culture **B**★) as its headquarters.
Festa de Sant Joan (night of the 23rd).
July
Festa del Grec: one of the city's most important cultural festivals: theater, dance, music, etc. (see www.bcn.es/grec)
August
Festa major de Gracia (around the 15th). Bals and concerts in the streets.
September
Festa Major de la Barceloneta (end Sep).
Festa de la Mercè;
Parade of the Giants and castellers (human pyramids).

24 HOURS IN BARCELONA

Breakfast
Not particularly early and not very substantial ... why not try thick hot chocolate and a delicious pastry at Granja Viader, a former dairy (**B** B3).
Lunch
Eaten around 2pm, never earlier. From noon, if you're peckish, drop into one of the many tapas bars for a plate or two of sizzling tapas to keep you going. Or sample the stalls in the covered markets of the Boqueria (**B** B4) or Sant Antoni (**E** D3). Between 2–4pm everything goes quiet: this is siesta time so seize the opportunity to have a snooze.
Dinner
Also eaten late: never before 9.30pm or 10pm. In the meantime, enjoy an early-evening glass of cava accompanied by anchovies on toast while you're waiting: El Xampanyet (**A** D1). Sample the Catalan specialties in the restaurants of the old city or in Barceloneta.
Nightlife
Around midnight visit the bars (in the Barrí Gótic or El Born) (**A** C-D-E-1) and then head for a trendy club in the Poble Espanyol (**E** B2) or those in L'Eixample (**C**). Insomniacs can always round the evening off around 6am with a late-night drink at Bar París (**D** A5), for example.

PARADE OF GIANTS

PUBLIC TELEPHONE

BOQUERIA MARKET

port goods), along with
the big Spanish names.
Triangle (B C2)
→ *Plaça de Catalunya, 1*
, 93 318 01 08 *(Mon-Sat)*
e most recent mall
99): FNAC, Habitat... and
zens of smart boutiques.
remagnum (**A** C3)
Moll d'Espanya
93 225 81 00
amazing shopping
ater right on the seafront.
ops, restaurants, cafés,
emas... Open until 11pm,
uding Sun.
celona Glòries (**F** D3)
Avinguda Diagonal, 208
93 486 04 04 *(Mon-Sat)*
largest shopping mall
pain: over 200 shops,
permarket, cinemas,
s and restaurants.
anish labels
nish brands are now
d throughout the world
they are usually up to
cheaper in Spain.
go (**D** B6)
asseig de Gràcia, 8-10
93 412 15 99 *(Mon-Sat)*

Fashion streetwear for
younger tastes.
Camper (B C3)
→ *Carrer Pelai, 13–37*
Tel. 93 302 41 24 *(Mon-Sat)*
Hardwearing, trendy shoes.
Six other branches
throughout Barcelona.
Zara (B C3)
→ *Carrer de Pelai, 58*
Tel. 93 301 09 78 *(Mon-Sat)*
Latest fashions from the
big design names, for all
tastes and all ages.
**Cheap and trendy
second-hand clothes**
Clothing to help you blend
in with clubbers and enjoy
that 'Barcelona style':
**@lternative Wear Club
(B** A-B3)
→ *Carrer de la Riera
Baixa, 4-6*
Tel. 93 443 90 11 *(Mon-Sat)*
Everything the younger
ones could possibly need
for the complete clubbing
outfit. The entire street is
along the same lines:
music, tattoos, body-
piercing and accessories.

El Mercadillo (B C3)
→ *Carrer de Portaferrissa, 17*
Tel. 93 301 89 13 *(Mon-Sat)*
Shopping gallery mostly
geared to clubwear. Faded
jeans, suede boots, lace
bodies and essential
accessories (bags, shades,
jewelry). All the shops here
are in a similar vein.

SHOWS

Reservations through:
FNAC (**B** C3; **C** B3)
→ *Plaça de Catalunya, 4*
Tel. 93 344 18 00 *(Mon-Sat)*
→ *Avinguda Diagonal, 549*
Tel. 93 444 59 00 *(Mon-Sat)*
Servicaixa
→ *Tel. 902 33 22 11 (Mon-Sat)*
By telephone or at
automatic ticket machines
in La Caixa banks, open
24 hours daily.
Tel.Entrada
→ *Tel. 902 10 12 12*
(93 479 99 20 from abroad)
Daily 8am–midnight
www.telentrada.com
By telephone or at Caixa

Catalunya banks.
Reductions
Tiquet −3 (**B** C3)
→ *Plaça de Catalunya, 17*
Tel. 902 10 12 12
Half-price seats, available
three hours before
performance.
Show information
Guía del Ocio
→ *Every Thu, 0.75 € from
newsstands*
Complete listings (films,
theater, concerts...).
Tentaciones
→ *Every Fri*
Friday supplement in the
Spanish newspaper
El País.
¿Qué fem?
→ *Every Fri*
Supplement in the Catalan
newspaper *La Vanguardia.*
Butxaca
→ *Monthly, free (in bars,
FNAC...)*
Listing of cultural events
(concerts, cinema, art,
arthouse cinema and
experimental video,
exhibitions...).

METRONÒM

MERCAT DEL BORN

MUSEU MARÍTIM

★ **Monestir Sant Pau del Camp** (**A** A1)
→ *Carrer de Sant Pau, 99*
Tel. 93 441 00 01
Mon, Wed-Sun 11.30am–1pm, 6–7.30pm; Thu 11.30am–1pm
In the 10th century, when the original church was built, El Raval was a remote area; today it is one of the city's most densely populated districts. This monastery, with its peaceful little cloister, is the oldest in Barcelona and a rare example of Romanesque architecture.

★ **Plaça Reial** (**A** C1)
Built between 1848 and 1859, this is one of Barcelona's busiest squares, often full of bongo-playing hippies. Plaça Reial is the only square in the city to be designed as a set piece and there is an extraordinary architectural unity as a result. The shady palm trees and the street-lamps (designed by the young Antonio Gaudí in 1878) which surround the Three Graces fountain help to soften the austere lines of the square's buildings. With covered passageways leading off it, this is a haven in the heart of the old city. There are shops and bars under the arcades.

★ **Palau Güell** (**A** B1)
→ *Carrer Nou de la Rambla, 3*
Tel. 93 317 39 74
Mon-Sat 10am–6.15pm; (visits by guided tour only)
All the hallmarks of Gaudí's genius are reunited here. From the ground floor to the chimneys the master juggled proportions and materials (iron, wood and mosaics) and played with color to produce what was his first major work (1889).

★ **Las Ramblas** (**A** B1)
Everyone who visits Barcelona comes to Las Ramblas first. It is touristy and the bars and restaurants are expens(and mostly not good), Las Ramblas is great fu nevertheless. Built on a riverbed which formed western boundary to th city until it dried up in 18th century, it is now splendid and lively str running from the Plaça Catalunya down to the seafront, with bars an cafés, buskers and sta Don't miss the wonde covered foodhall halfv down on the right.

★ **Basílica Santa Ma del Mar** (**A** D1)
→ *Plaça de Santa Mario Daily 9am–1.30pm, 4.3 A good example of Ca*

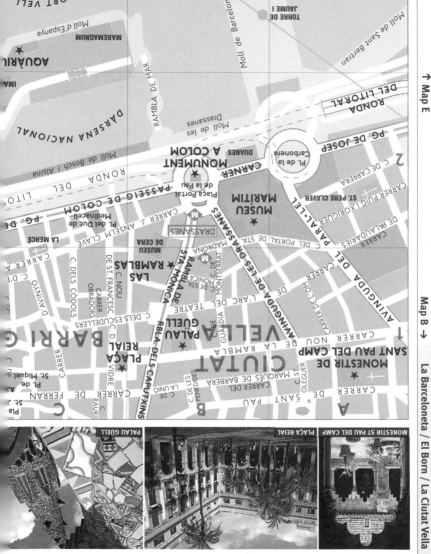

PALAU GÜELL

PLAÇA REIAL

MONESTIR ST PAU DEL CAMP

Barcelona oberta al mar, Barcelona faces toward the sea... To the south of Las Ramblas, from La Barceloneta and El Born, the salty tang in the air is a constant reminder of the nearby ocean. The waterfront was completely transformed for the 1992 Olympics and the revamped coastal area is now reminiscent of Marseilles or Naples. El Born, the latest place to be seen for Barcelona's fashion-conscious inhabitants contains some restored medieval gems, while all over La Barceloneta (Little Barcelona) you find evidence of the city's rich seafaring and fishing heritage, which has diminished but is far from forgotten.

ANTIGA CASA SOLÉ
BAR HIVERN

RESTAURANTS

Senyor Parellada (**A** D1)
→ *Carrer de l'Argenteria, 37*
Tel. 93 310 50 94
Daily 1–3.30pm, 8–midnight
Delicious Catalan specialties and dishes of the day have won this restaurant its good reputation. All served in a charming setting, spread over two levels, around a glass-covered courtyard. À la carte 18 €.

Cal Pep (**A** E1)
→ *Plaça de les Olles, 8*
Tel. 93 310 79 61
Mon–Sat 1.30–3.30pm, 8pm–midnight (closed Mon lunch and in Aug)
Cal Pep presides at the bar, where an eager line of regulars enjoy tapas dishes (tasty Spanish bar snacks) such as fried baby cuttlefish, *gambas a la plancha* (grilled shrimp), clams and baby peppers. You will probably need to wait your turn. Sip a glass of chilled white wine and hope that a place at the bar becomes free before too long. Around 20 €.

Salero (**A** E1)
→ *Carrer del Rec, 60*
Tel. 93 319 80 22
Mon–Sat 1.30–4pm, 9pm–2am (3am Fri-Sat)
White walls, tasteful music and a menu that is imaginative without being showy. The menu changes regularly and often uses Mediterranean ingredients to cook foreign dishes. One thing never changes though: it always includes (very fresh) fish. À la carte 21 €.

7 Portes (**A** D1)
→ *Passeig d'Isabel II, 14*
Tel. 93 319 30 33
Daily 1pm–1am
In business since 1836, this restaurant attracts tourists and locals alike. Paella with *escalivada* (a mixture of peppers and eggplant) is always a safe bet. Fast, efficient service. À la carte 35 €.

Antiga Casa Solé (**A** D3)
→ *Carrer Sant Carles, 4*
Tel. 93 221 50 12
Tue-Sun 1–4pm, 8–11pm
A favorite haunt of the Barcelonese, Antiga Casa Solé is found hidden away from the more touristy main street which runs along the coast. It serves what are, without doubt, the best rice and seafood dishes in the city: black rice (with cuttlefish ink), rice *caldoso* (a type of soup with rice).
À la carte 42 €.

EL XAMPANYET

EL INGENIO

CAFÉS, TAPAS

Tèxtil Cafè (A D1)
→ Carrer de Montcada, 12
Tel. 93 268 25 98
Tue-Sun 10am–midnight
Located in a splendid
medieval palace which
also houses the Textile
Museum, this café opens
onto a gorgeous Gothic
patio terrace. The perfect
setting for breakfast or a
light lunch.

Cafè Schilling (A C1)
→ Carrer de Ferran, 23
Tel. 93 317 67 87
Mon-Sat 10am–3am;
Sun noon–2.30am
Of Barcelona's many
fashionable cafés,
Schilling was the first.
Usually packed full,
with a cozy atmosphere,
old-fashioned décor – this
is still the perfect place for
a get-together over a drink
and a snack: bocadillos
(sandwiches), pastries,
bollos (croissants).

El Xampanyet (A D1)
→ Carrer de Montcada, 22
Tel. 93 319 70 03
Tue-Sat noon–4pm, 6.30–
11.30pm; Sun noon–4pm.
Closed in Aug
Pronounce 'champanyet'.
The greatest tapas bar in
the city has been in the
Esteve family for three
generations. People come
here for the anchovies

(served in a sauce
– a secret recipe of the
house), and the cider and
chilled cava (Spanish
champagne). Tasty tapas
from 1€ to 2€.

La Vinya
del Senyor (A D1)
→ Carrer Santa Maria, 5
Tel. 93 310 33 79
Tue-Thu noon–1am (2am
Fri-Sat; midnight Sun)
The terrace of this
traditional bodega
spills out onto the plaza
of the Basilica Santa
Maria del Mar. Selected
wines, sherries and
dessert wines, along with
tasty, good quality, ham
and cheese tapas dishes.

BARS, CLUBS

Bar Hivernacle (A E1)
→ Passeig de Picasso (in
the Parc de la Ciutadella)
Tel. 93 295 40 17
Mon-Sat 9.30am–midnight;
Sun 9.30am–4pm
This is a greenhouse
that has been
imaginatively converted
into a restaurant. Here
you will find exotic
plants, jazz musicians
(Wednesday evenings)
or classical music, lovers
dining by candlelight or
friends in conversation
over a glass of wine.
The décor is gorgeous,

particularly at night,
when the dome is prettily
illuminated.

Bar Pastís (A B1)
→ Carrer Santa Mònica, 4
Tel. 93 318 79 80
Tue-Sun 7.30pm–2.30am
You'll only find two
tables and eight stools
in this 90-sq-ft space:
flowing pastis, French
music... for over 50 years
this has been the place
to find a taste of France
in the Catalan capital.
Tango dancing on Sunday.

Astin (A D1)
→ Carrer Abaixadors, 9
Tel. 93 310 10 58
Thu-Sat 10pm–3am
Nitsaclub's (E D4) little
brother. One comes here
to have a drink while
listening to the best DJs
in the city (from 11pm
onward).

SHOPPING

La Manual
Alpargatera (A C1)
→ Carrer d'Avinyó, 7
Tel. 93 301 01 72 /Mon-Sat
9.30am–1.30pm, 4.30–8pm
John Paul II and Jeanne
Moreau are both loyal
customers of this shop's
hand-made espadrilles
which come in every
color and style, from
traditional to the truly
outlandish. From 5 €.

Indumentària (A C1)
→ Carrer d'Avinyó, 18
Tel. 93 301 00 06
Mon-Sat 10.30am–2pm,
4.30–8.30pm
Catalan stylists famous for
their quality fabrics and
designs to match. More
expensive than anywhere
else, but infinitely more
original. In the same vein,
at n°12 and n°50 are Tribu
and Zsu-Zsa selling
imaginative designs. Works
by young artists hang on
the walls.

Legendary shops
El Ingenio (A C1)
→ Carrer Rauric, 6
Tel. 93 317 71 38
Has sold masks, balloons
and assorted tricks since
1838.

Casa Gispert (A D1)
→ Carrer dels Sombrerers,
23 / Tel. 93 319 75 35
Coffee, dried fruit, cocoa,
spices, dried mushrooms...
all prepared in-house
since 1851.

Arlequí Màscares (A D1)
→ Carrer Princesa 7
Tel. 93 268 27 52
Mon-Sat 10.30am–8pm;
Sun 10am–4pm
Hand-crafted masks and
puppets in papier mâché
representing characters
from popular Catalan tales,
the Commedia dell'arte
or Noh theater – real works
of art.

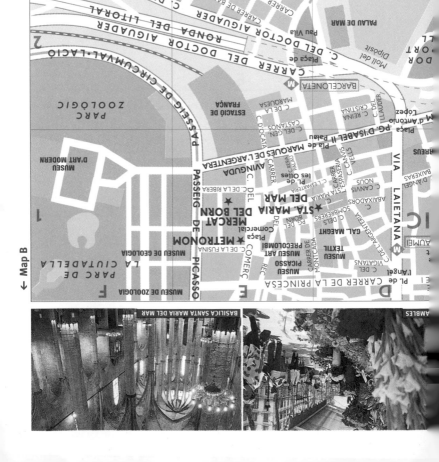

BASILICA SANTA MARIA DEL MAR

AMBLES

← Map B

PARC DE
LA CIUTADELLA

MUSEU DE GEOLOGIA

MUSEU DE ZOOLOGIA

PARC
ZOOLOGIC

MUSEU
D'ART MODERN

PASSEIG DE CIRCUMVAL·LACIÓ

CARRER DEL DOCTOR AIGUADER

RONDA DEL LITORAL

C. DEL DOCTOR AIGUADER

↑ Map F

LA BARCELONETA

PARC DE LA
BARCELONETA

HOSPITAL
DEL MAR

CARRER D'ANDREA DORIA

CARRER SANT CARLES

PASSEIG MARITIM DE LA BARCELONETA

CARRER ALMIRALL

PASSEIG JOAN DE BORBÓ

Moll de la Barceloneta

MARINA

PALAU DE MAR

C. DE GINEBRA

CARRER DE BALBOA

C. DE LA
MAQUINISTA

Pau Vila

Plaça de

Moll del
Dipòsit

PORT
VELL

Moll d'
DOR...

BARCELONETA Ⓜ

ESTACIÓ DE
FRANÇA

C. DOCTIA

C. DE LA
MARQUESA

C. DEL GEN.
CASTAÑOS

C. DE LA
REINA CRISTINA

C. DEL
LLAUDER

Plaça de
M d'Antonio
López

Pg. D'ISABEL II

Pla de MARQUES DE L'ARGENTERA

AVINGUDA

Pla de Palau

C. DE LA RIBERA

PASSEIG DE PICASSO

C. DEL COMERÇ

COMERÇ

C. DE LA FUSINA

REC

CARRER DE MONTCADA

MUSEU
PICASSO

MUSEU ART
PRECOLOMBÍ

MUSEU
TÈXTIL

Plaça
Comercial

MERCAT DEL BORN

STA. MARIA DEL MAR ★

★ METROMON

MONUMON

PG. DEL
BORN

C. DELS
SOMBRERERS

GAL. MAEGHT

C. DE L'ARGENTERIA

CARRER DE LA PRINCESA

C. VIGATANS

L'Àngel

C. DEL
Pl. de
Pl. de
l'Àngel

JAUME Ⓜ

VIA LAIETANA

D'ANGEL BAIXERAS

ABAIXADORS

C. CANVIS
NOUS

C. CANVIS
VELLS

C. ESPARTERIA

CARRER
ESPASERIA VIS.

CARRERA
STA MARIA

C. DE LA
CARRERA

PL. de
les Olles

REUS

ABLES

Sant Sebastià

MAR MEDITERRÁNIA

4

D   E   F

ARIUM

LA BARCELONETA

ic architecture. Built in 55 years (1329–84), basilica has an edible harmony. delicacy of the pillars porting the three naves tes a good sense of e. The exceptional stics make this the ect setting for concerts.

Barceloneta (A E3) tween Passeig Joan de 5 and Passeig Marítim build-up of sediment- against the harbor (1640) gradually gave o a triangular-shaped of land which was gnet for the city's less. In 1749, due gressive urban planning, it was torn down and replaced with a grid pattern of tiny houses for 10,000 fishermen and dockers. A friendly and cheap district. Good fish restaurants.

★ **Aquàrium (A** C3)
→ Moll d'Espanya, Port Vell
Daily 9.30am–9pm (9.30pm Sat-Sun; 11pm in July-Aug)
The largest aquarium in Europe. Manta ray, sea horses, moonfish, moray eels and octopus: the entire range of Mediterranean basin sea-life.

★ **Museu Marítim (A** B2)/
Monument a Colom (A B2)
→ Avinguda de
les Drassanes

Daily 10am–7pm
At the foot of Las Ramblas stands the statue of Columbus (1888), pointing out to sea, in homage to the famous explorer who, on his return from the New World, came here to present himself to the Spanish sovereign and be loaded with honors. Opposite is the Drassanes, the 13th-century medieval shipyards, now a maritime museum with a unique collection of model vessels, maps and a 16th-century Royal Galley.

★ **Mercat del Born (A** E1)
→ Plaça Comercial, 12
This once housed the largest market in Barcelona

(it transferred to Montjuïc in the 1970s). The huge deserted market-hall is a fine example of 19th century Spanish metal-and-glass architecture. A library is being built within its walls.

★ **Metronóm (A** E1)
→ Carrer de la Fusina, 9
Tel. 93 268 42 98
Tue-Sat 11am–2pm,
5–8.30pm. Closed August
A good venue for alternative artistic events. Under the Art Deco-style dome you will find photography exhibitions, multi-media installations, experimental music, art and video.

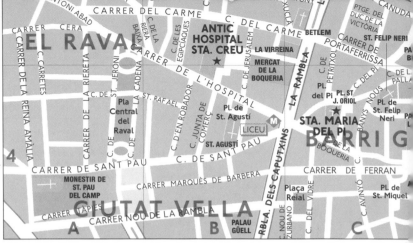

CATEDRAL

MUSEU D'HISTÒRIA DE LA CIUTAT

PLAÇA SANT JAUME

★ Museu d'Art Contemporani de Barcelona (MACBA) (B B3)

→ Plaça dels Àngels, 1
Tel. 93 412 08 10
Mon, Wed-Fri 11am–8pm;
Sat 10am–8pm; Sun and
public hols 10am–3pm
In the heart of El Raval, in
an ever-changing working-
class area, stands a
striking, spotless building
designed by Richard Meier
in 1995. It houses a major
contemporary art museum,
which mounts temporary
exhibitions of the latest
trends in Catalan and
contemporary
international art.

★ Centre de Cultura Contemporània de Barcelona (CCCB) (B B3)

→ Carrer de Montalegre, 5
Tel. 93 306 41 00
Tue, Thu-Fri 11am–2pm,
4–8pm; Wed, Sat 11am–8pm
and public hols 11am–7pm
The remarkable restoration
work undertaken here has
turned a former orphanage
into a modern space. This
center juggles different
artistic disciplines and
mounts a variety of
exhibitions and activities.

★ Palau de la Música Catalana (B D3)

→ Carrer Sant Francesc de
Paula, 2
Daily 10am–5.30pm

This spectacular Modernist
building was designed by
Domènech i Montaner and
completed in 1908. The
façade, with its multi-
colored mosaic-covered
pillars, hints at the
extraordinary richness
of the interior, whose
stained-glass windows and
inverted polychrome glass
dome bathe the concert
hall in a soft light.

★ Antic Hospital de la Santa Creu (B B3)

→ Carrer de l'Hospital, 56
Tue-Sat noon–2pm, 4pm–
8pm; Sun 11am–2pm (chapel)
The eclectic talent of young
Barcelonese artists has
been given a home in the

This spectacular Modernist
Gothic chapel of this
former hospital (1401).
Magnificent patio.

★ Santa Maria del Pi Plaça Sant Josep Ori (B C4)

→ Between Plaça del Pi
Plaça Sant Josep Oriol
Daily 8.30am–1pm,
4.30–9pm
The Gothic basilica of
Santa Maria del Pi (14t
century) would be noth
exceptional were it not
the scale of its central
nave, one of the larges
be found in any Catala
church. The surroundi
squares make for a
pleasant walk. An art
market is held on the

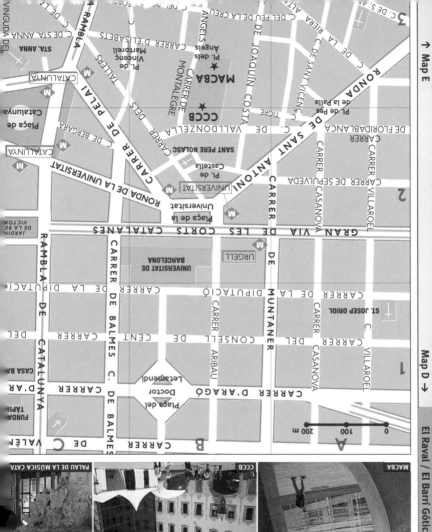

PALAU DE LA MÚSICA CATA...

CCCB

MACBA

Representing the city in miniature, these three districts overflow with the elements that make up the true magic of Barcelona: the narrow, disreputable streets of El Raval; the Catalan Gothic architectural gems around the cathedral; and the restored mansions in the old bourgeois district of La Ribera. During the day traditional shops and covered markets draw crowds of tourists and locals alike, with their friendly atmosphere and colorful hustle and bustle. At night the historic heart of the city comes alive, with its numerous tiny bars, trendy clubs and cheap restaurants providing the entertainment.

SILENUS

GRANJA M. VIADER

RESTAURANTS

Romesco (**B** B4)
→ Carrer de Sant Pau, 28
Tel. 93 318 93 81
Mon–Sat 1pm–midnight
Family cooking at reasonable prices, a few yards from Las Ramblas. Specialties include *frijoles* (kidney beans). À la carte 8 €.

Madrid-Barcelona (**B** D1)
→ Carrer d'Aragó, 282
Tel. 93 215 70 27 / Mon-Sat 1–4pm, 8.30– midnight
Has a reputation built on its excellent seafood tapas and traditional dishes, prepared using market-fresh ingredients. À la carte 15–22 €.

Casa Alfonso (**B** D2)
→ Roger de Lluría, 6
Tel. 93 301 97 83
Mon-Tue 9am–10pm; Wed–Fri 9am–1am
This charcutería, next to the Urquinaona square, has been around since 1934. Book ahead if you want to eat in the room at the back, otherwise there are a few seats at the counter. Great surroundings – hanging hams, glass cabinets and wall paintings. Delicious tapas. À la carte 15–22 €.

Salsitas (**B** B4)
→ Carrer Nou de la Rambla, 22
Tel. 93 318 08 40 / Daily 8pm–midnight (bar until 3am)
The stark white décor provides a backdrop to the lavish world cuisine. Eclectic crowd and techno music with video shows. À la carte 28 €.

Taxidermista (**B** C4)
→ Plaça Reial, 8
Tel. 93 412 45 36 Tue-Sun 1.30–4pm, 8.30pm–midnight
Superbly refurbished restaurant in the former Natural Science Museum, under the arches of Plaça Reial. Modern cuisine prepared using local produce: *cigales del mar* (crab) with *escalivada*, cod with *piquillo* peppers, fries made from yams. Menu 30€.

Silenus (**B** B3)
→ Carrer Àngels, 8
Tel. 93 302 26 80
Mon-Sat 1.30–4pm, 8.30–11.30pm (midnight Fri-Sat)
The high ceilings and white walls dotted with works by local artists make Silenus a haven in the heart of El Raval. Imaginative cuisine offering the best Catalan and Spanish dishes. À la carte 40 €.

Casa Leopoldo (**B** B4)
→ Carrer de Sant Rafael, 24
Tel. 93 441 69 42
Tue-Sat 1.30–4pm, 9–11pm; Sun 1.30–4pm. Closed in Au
This venerable establishment, which has been in

PALOMA

ESCRIBA

EL MANANTIAL DE SALUD

the Gil family since 1929, is located in a small street in the Barrí Xino and is a famous haunt of Pepe Carvalho, hero of the detective novels by Vázquez Montalbán. Specialties: fish of the day, cooked *a la plancha* (grilled), tripe and fried squid. À la carte 45 €.

CAFÉS, TAPAS

Granja M. Viader (B B3)
→ *Carrer Xuclà, 4–6*
Tel. 93 318 34 86
Tue-Sat 9am–1.45pm,
5–8.30pm; Mon 5–7.30pm
Whipped cream, *mel i mató* (honey and fromage frais), rich hot chocolate and *suizos* (a type of donut)... Stop at this dairy for breakfast or a quiet afternoon tea away from the buzz of Las Ramblas and the bustle of the Boqueria marketplace.

Bar Pinotxo (B B4)
→ *Mercat de la Boqueria, 66–67 / Tel. 93 317 17 31*
Mon-Sat 6am–4pm
The most animated kiosk in the market, with a band of followers who keep coming back for the *langostinos a la plancha* (grilled baby crawfish) and *codornices* (quail). Stand with your back to the fruit and vegetable stalls to

see the colorful spectacle of Catalan dishes being prepared in front of the hungry but happy line of customers waiting at the counter.

Caelum (B C4)
→ *Carrer de la Palla, 8*
Tel. 93 302 69 93
Tue-Sun 1–8.30pm (9pm Sat); Mon 5–8.30pm
Temptation under the roof of these former Jewish baths (14th century). Sample the specialties produced in the convents and monasteries of Spain: *yemas* (made with egg yolk, sugar and almond), *turrón de la abuela* (nougat in dark chocolate) and much more.

BARS, CLUBS, SHOWS

Boadas Cocktail Bar (B C3)
→ *Carrer del Tallers, 1*
Tel. 93 318 88 26 / Daily noon–2am (3am Fri-Sat)
A small bar, open since 1933 and very close to La Rambla. Warm atmosphere, a clientele of locals, mostly, and very good, original, cocktails; top marks for the excellent *mojitos*.

London Bar (B B4)
→ *Carrer Nou de la Rambla, 34*

Tel. 93 318 52 61
Tue-Sun 7.30pm–4.30am (5pm Fri-Sat)
Without question, this bar is in a category of its own: all ages, all trends, all types of music. Concerts and shows every evening.

Café Royale (B C4)
→ *Carrer Nou de Zurbano, 3 / Tel. 93 317 61 24*
Sun-Thu 5.30pm–0.30am (3am Fri-Sat)
When it opened four years ago Café Royale became quickly *the* place to be. It has aged well and remains a firm favorite among clubbers. Two different spaces (a bar and a lounge area with DJ) still cater to the latest trends in Barcelona.

La Paloma (B A2)
→ *Carrer Tigre, 27*
Tel. 93 301 68 97
Thu-Sat 6–9.30pm;
Thu 11pm–4am;
Fri 11pm–5am;
Sat 11.30pm–5am;
Sun 5.45–9.45pm
The older inhabitants of the district, those who remember this splendid ballroom in its heyday, faithfully return here to attend the afternoon tea dance, gliding around the floor to the *paso doble* and the cha-cha-cha. In the evening the establish-

ment is taken over by the younger generation and becomes a nightclub specializing in techno music.

Círcol Maldà (B C4)
→ *Carrer del Pi, 5*
Tel. 93 412 43 86
Call for the program
The spirit of the literary salon still presides here in this 17th-century palace, where groups meet on Thu evenings (sometimes other days too: call for info). Literary evenings, concerts, debates. Charming, elegant atmosphere.

SHOPPING

Escriba (B C3)
→ *La Rambla, 83*
Tel. 93 301 60 27
Daily 9am–9pm
This famous patisserie is known for its wonderful Modernist façade and its delicious chocolates and cookies.

Herbolari El Manantial de Salud (B B3)
→ *Carrer Xuclà, 23*
Tel. 93 301 14 44
Mon-Sat 9am–2pm, 4–8pm
The most authentic herbalist in Barcelona. Its old cupboards are packed with plants from all over the world. In-store preparation of perfumed oils and all kinds of healing potions.

PLAÇA SANT JOSEP ORIOL

ANTIC HOSPITAL DE LA SANTA CREU

← Map F

↑ Map F

← Map D

EL FORT PIUS

Plaça de Tetuan

Plaça d'Urquinaona

PALAU DE LA MÚSICA CATALANA

CENTRE CULTURAL FUNDACIÓ LA CAIXA

GRAN VIA DE LES CORTS CATALANES

M URQUINAONA
M ARC DE TRIOMF
M TETUAN
M GIRONA

AVINGUDA DE VILANOVA

CARRER DE VALÈNCIA
CARRER D'ARAGÓ
CARRER DE CONSELL DE CENT
CARRER DE LA DIPUTACIÓ
CARRER D'AUSIAS MARC
RONDA DE ST. PERE
CARRER DE ST. PERE MÉS

PASSEIG DE SANT JOAN
PASSEIG DE GRÀCIA

CARRER DE ROGER DE FLOR
CARRER DE BAILÈN
CARRER DE GIRONA
CARRER DEL BRUC
CARRER DE PAU CLARIS
CARRER DE ROGER DE LLÚRIA

C. D'ORTIGOSA
C. DE MÉNDEZ NÚÑEZ
C. DE ST. PERE MÉS ALT
ST. PERE
C. DE LES MOLES
C. DE COMTAL

CARRER D'ALÍ BEI
CARRER DE TRAFALGAR

PLAÇA TANELLA
ARRER TANELLA
LLÚRIA

1   2   3
D   E   F

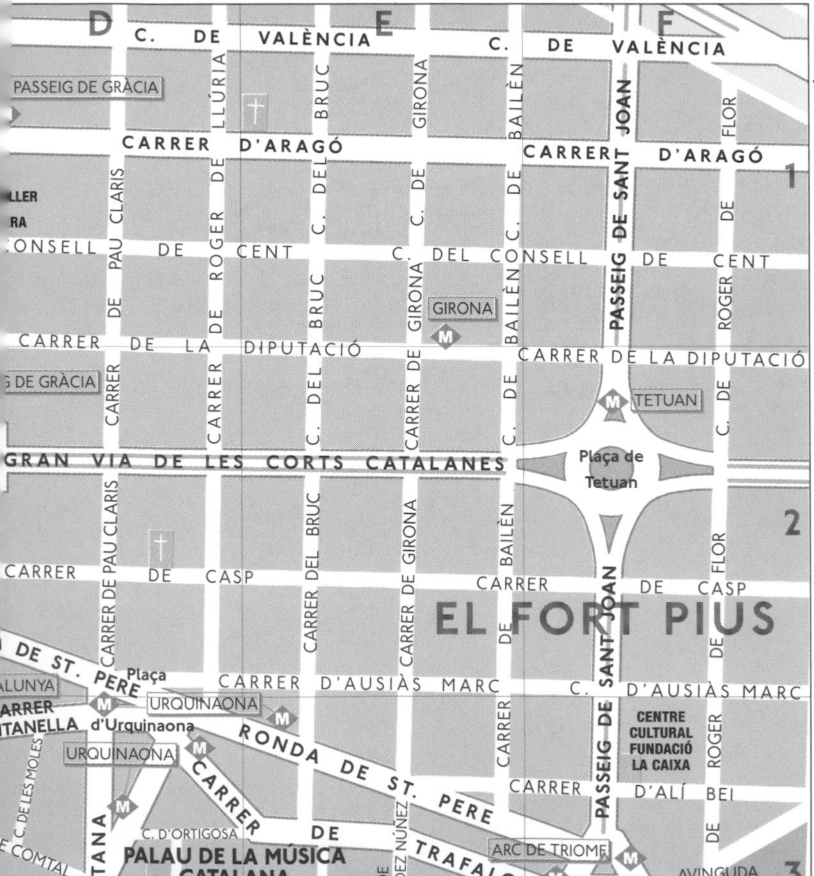

LA RIBERA

VIA LAIETANA

MONTSIÓ

CARRER DE ST. PERE MÉS BAIX

DE LES PUEL·LES

CARRER DEL ALT

ARC DEL TRIOMF

C. DELS GRISTANS

NGUDA DE CATEDRAL

AVINGUDA DE F. CAMBÓ

C. D'EN LLÀSTICS

CARRER DEL PORTAL NOU

PASSEIG DE

LLUÍS COMPANYS

CARRER DELS ALMOGÀVERS

PALAU DE JUSTICIA

SA DE L'ARDIACA

CATEDRAL

Pl. del Rei

C. D'EN GIRALT EL PELLISSER

Pl. de St. Augustí Vell

CARRER DELS CARDERS

C. D'EN TANTARANTANA

CARRER DE BUENAVENTURA MUÑOZ

MUSEU D'HISTORIA
★ DE LA CIUTAT

IC

CARRER BÒRIA

C. D'EN COMERÇ

PASSEIG DE PUJADES

AÇA
JAUME
E JAUME I

VIA LAIETANA

C. DE L'ARGENTERIA

CARRER DE LA PRINCESA

JAUME I

MUSEU TÈXTIL

★ MUSEU PICASSO

★ CARRER MONTCADA

C. MONTCADA

C. DEL

PASSEIG DE PICASSO

MUSEU DE ZOOLOGIA

MUSEU DE GEOLOGIA

PARC DE LA CIUTADELLA

4

Map A →

Pl. de t. Just

GAL. MAEGHT

METRONOM

D

E

F

MAEGHT

MUSEU PICASSO

CARRER MONTCADA

---

kend of each month.
rrer Montcada (B E4)
e medieval mansion
ses, which run the
h of the street, were
home to Barcelona's
thiest merchants and
ow museums and art
ries: Galerie Maeght,
eu Tèxtil and, next
the Museu Barbier-
ler (with its pre-
nbian art).
useu Picasso (B E4)
rrer Montcada, 15
B 319 63 10 / Tue-Sat
–8pm (3pm Sun)
alau Berenguer
ilar contains the
so Museum. The core
collection is the

master's early works and
several buildings adjacent
to the small palace have
also been taken over
to house the masses of
sketches, drawings and
paintings produced by the
prolific young artist. See
here the outstanding Las
Meninas series, variations
on the Velázquez painting.
★ **Plaça St Jaume (B** D4)
It is not by chance that the
city hall and the Palau de
la Generalitat have been
situated here since the
14th century. Dating back
to Roman times this was
the site of the crossroads
of the city's two major
thoroughfares. The

baroque salons of the city
hall are well worth seeing.
★ **Museu d'Història
de la Ciutat (B** D4)
➔ Plaça del Rei
Tel. 93 315 11 11
Tue-Sat 10am–2pm, 4–8pm
(10am–8pm in summer);
Sun 10am–2pm
A superb tribute to the
history of Barcelona, with
collections of drawings and
documents describing the
development of the city.
Underground, spread over
4,784 sq yds, are the
remains of the ancient
Roman city of Barcino.
★ **Catedral (B** D4)
➔ Plaça de la Seu / Daily
8am–1.30pm, 5–7.30pm

Santa Lucia chapel is the
only reminder of the original
Romanesque church
(9th century), although
some elements have been
incorporated into the
present cathedral (1298–
1450). The spire and façade
were not completed until
the early 20th century, yet
the building emanates an
atmosphere of great
harmony and style. The
nave, edged with chapels,
the choir, decorated with
finely carved stalls and the
cloisters are good examples
of pure Catalan-Gothic. The
Catalan dance, the sardana,
takes place in front of the
cathedral on Sun mornings.

PALAU DE PEDRALBES

COLLEGI DE LES TERESIANES

← Map E

A

B

C

★ Jardins de la Villa Cecília / Parc de la Quinta Amèlia (C B2)
➜ *Carrer de Santa Amèlia Daily 10am–6pm (7pm March and Oct; 8pm April and Sep; 9pm May–Aug)*
On one side of the Carrer Santa Amèlia, a small ordinary-looking street, are the gardens of the Villa Cecília – a maze of tall hedges containing a curious bronze sculpture of a drowning woman. On the other side of the street is the more traditional Quinta Amèlia park, with a pond in the centre and benches scattered here and there.

★ Monestir de Pedralbes (C B1)
➜ *Baixada del Monestir, 9 Tel. 93 280 14 34 Tue-Sun 10am–2pm*
Part of the Thyssen-Bornemisza collection (the bulk of which is in Madrid) has, since 1993, occupied the former sleeping quarters and main salon of the apartments of Queen Elisenda. Founded in 1326, this Catalan Gothic-style convent has been occupied by members of the Poor Clares order ever since the 14th century.

★ Finca Güell (C A2)
➜ *Avinguda de Pedralbes, 7*
A ferocious dragon guards the estate which Eusebi Güell entrusted to Gaudí for restoration in 1884. Drawing on the fashionable neo-Mudejar style, Gaudí redesigned the lodge, the stables and the gate linking the two buildings. Splendid crafted ironwork.

★ Palau de Pedralbes (C A2)
➜ *Avinguda Diagonal, 686 Tel. 93 280 13 64 Museums: Tue-Sun 10–6pm Garden: daily 10am–sunset*
Two interesting museums housed in a former palace (1919) which was inspired by Italian Renaissance mansions. Catalan, medieval-style decoration and furniture (Museum of Decorative Arts) and an exceptional collection of Spanish ceramics and medieval pottery (Ceramic Museum). In the park there is a splendid bank of fountains designed by Gaudí .

★ Collegi de les Teresianes (C D2)
➜ *Carrer de Ganduxer, 85–105 / Tel. 93 212 33 Sat-Sun 11am–1pm (by)*
Behind the huge brick façade lies a rich inter patios, parabolic-arche corridors and stairway Putting aside the eco and stylistic constrain imposed by the order

LES CORTS

TRAVESSERA DE LES CORTS

TRAVESSERA DE LES CORTS

DT. BENÍTEZ F. PAZ

A CARRER F. BENÍTEZ PAZ

LES CORTS M

TRAVE

C. DE GALILEU

C. DEL REMEI

C. DE JOAN GÜELL

GÜELL

C. DE MASFERRER

C. LES CORTS

C. DE GANDESA

GRAN VIA

CARLES III

NOU CAMP ★

C. DE LA MATERNITAT

C. DE S. ARANA

MARIA CRISTINA M

AVINGUDA DE JOAN XXIII

CEMENTIRI

AVINGUDA

CARRER MARTÍ FRANQUÈS

DIAGO

Dr. Pl. Reina M. Cristina

M

AVINGUDA

Plaça de Pius XII

LES CORTS

Dr. CARRER FERRAN

CARRER DEL DR. FERRAN

PASSEIG DE MANUEL GIRONA

C. DEL CAPT.

C. DE BELTRAN I RÓZPIDE

MUSEU CARROSSES

AVINGUDA DIAGONAL

PALAU REIAL M

PARC DE PEDRALBES

PARC I QUINTA

C. D'EDUARDO CONDE

C. MARQUÈS DE

AVINGUDA DE PEDRALBES

PALAU DE PEDRALBES

2

DE JORDI GIRONA

PARC DEL CARDENAL

MUSEU ETNOGRÀFIC ANDINO AMAZÒNIC

C. DE BOSCH I GIMPERA

C. DE MUHACÉN

AVINGUDA DE PEDRALBES

FINCA GÜELL ★

Plaça d'eusebi Güell

PEDRALBES

JAI DE L.

C. DR. F. DARDER

C. DR. FER.

CARRER DE SOR EULÀLIA D'ANZU

CARRER DELS CAVALLERS

CARRER DELS

C. DE L'ABADESSA OLZET

CARRETERA D'ESPLUGUES

DE MIRET I SANS

RONDA DE DALT B20

MONESTIR DE PEDRALBES ★

C. DEL BISBE CATALÀ

CARRER DEL MONESTIR

C. DE MONTEVIDEO

B

DETAIL OF GATE – FINCA GÜELL

JARDINS DE LA VILLA CECÍLIA

MONESTIR DE PEDRALBES

Sarrià / Pedralbes / Sants

Situated around the imposing, seemingly endless Avinguda Diagonal, the busy, commercial thoroughfare running northwest to southeast across Barcelona, the villages of Sarrià, Pedralbes and Sants are now mainly residential areas. In Sarrià the atmosphere is largely that of an exclusive provincial town (the best schools are here), especially in the residential back streets away from the main drag. The monumental Pedralbes ('the white stones'), complete with palace and gardens, is on the west side and runs to the city limits. Sants is more sparsely populated and features a modern railway station.

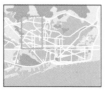

EL VELL SARRIÀ A CONTRALUZ

RESTAURANTS

Bene Asai (**C** D2)
→ *Carrer del Doctor Carulla, 61 / Tel. 93 434 06 77*
Daily 1.30–4pm, 8.30–11.30pm. Closed August
Tiny restaurant especially popular with the younger local crowd. Good Italian specialties (pasta and pizza) prepared by a Genoese chef. In summer, eat outside on the terrace.
À la carte 15 €.

La Vaquería (**C** C4)
→ *Carrer de Deu i Mata, 141 Tel. 93 419 07 35*
Mon-Fri 1.30–4pm, 9pm–0.30am; Sat 9pm–0.30am
Three different areas with three distinct moods, in a tastefully refurbished cowshed: piano-bar, disco and unpretentious restaurant, whose gamble to offer imaginative, tasty fare in an unusual setting (at a good price), has certainly paid off. Set menus: 13 € (lunch), 22 € (dinner).

Friends (**C** C4)
→ *Carrer de Deu i Mata, 126 Tel. 93 439 35 56*
Mon (dinner)-Sat (lunch) 1–5pm, 7.30pm-midnight
The family cooking draws a faithful following of diners who enjoy the relaxed, friendly atmosphere and warm welcome. Piano player on Friday evenings. Set lunch menu 10 €.
À la carte 25 €.

El Vell Sarrià (**C** C1)
→ *Carrer Major de Sarrià 93 Tel. 93 204 57 10*
Mon-Sat 1.30–3.30pm, 9–11.30pm; Sun 1.30–3.30pm
Sarrià has retained its provincial atmosphere, and this restaurant, in a house typical of the area, is probably the best establishment of its kind in the district, situated in a back alley away from the more touristy streets. Catalan, rice-based specialties with seasonal variations: mountain rice with mushrooms (with rabbit and *butifarra* – Catalan sausage cooked in white wine), rice with cod and baby vegetables, artichoke risotto, *cigales del mar* (crab), shrimp and mushrooms.
À la carte 28 €.

Negro (**C** C3)
→ *Avinguda Diagonal, 640 Tel. 93 405 94 44*
Daily 1.30–3pm, 8.30pm–1am (2am Fri-Sun)
Restaurant with New York designer décor. The cooking combines Mediterranean ingredients with Oriental know-how: Japanese-style chicken kebabs,

BAR TOMÁS

TRES TORRES

FOIX DE SARRIÀ

tuna fish *tartare*, cured spiced beef, Indian rice. À la carte 35 €.

Acontraluz (C D2)
→ *Carrer Milanesat, 19*
Tel. 93 203 06 58
Daily 1.30–5pm, 9pm–midnight (1am Fri-Sat)
The most fashionable terrace in town, complete with trailing jasmine and little candles. Seasonal cuisine, modern Mediterranean in style. Vegetables, risottos and desserts, all utterly delicious. À la carte 40 €.

CAFÉS, TAPAS

Bar Tomás (C C2)
→ *Carrer Major de Sarrià, 49 / Tel. 93 203 10 77*
Thu-Tue 8am–10pm
Closed August
Everyone in Barcelona agrees: the best *patatas bravas* (fried potato in a spicy sauce) to be found in the city are those on the menu at Bar Tomàs. Crisp and crunchy on the outside, soft on the inside and served with perfect sauces. The bar is always packed. *Patatas bravas* and beer, 2.25 €.

Tejada (C D4)
→ *Carrer del Tenor Viñas, 3*
Tel. 93 200 73 41
Daily 9am–1.30am
Closed 15 days in August

With a garden close by, this bar is an essential stop-off for its huge tapas menu and the bustle that seems to prevail day and night.

CLUBS, DISCOS

Tres Torres (C C1)
→ *Via Augusta, 300*
Tel. 93 205 10 37
Mon-Sat 7pm–3am
This magnificent Modernist tower escaped the bulldozer and has become a landmark for Barcelonese nightlife. A variety of styles stretch between the disco-bar and the superb terrace, which is open even in winter. This is where the city's rich kids hang out. Cocktail 6 €.

La Boîte (C D4)
→ *Avinguda Diagonal, 477*
Tel. 93 319 17 89
Daily 11.30pm–5.30am
This club attracts a fun-loving crowd looking for a good time to another sound than techno. Live bands (funk, soul, blues and hip-hop) in the early evening.

Bikini (C C4)
→ *Carrer de Deu i Mata, 105*
Tel. 93 322 00 05
Tue-Sun midnight–5am
Famous club which has now reopened but is

sticking to the formula which made it popular in the first place: one room is devoted to 1980s and 1990s music, another offers Latin rhythms for you to sway to, while the bar is an ideal place to sit and sip cocktails accompanied by nibbles.

Up & Down (C C3)
→ *Carrer de Numància, 179*
Tel. 93 205 51 94
Tue-Sat midnight–6am
Up: a restaurant and private club where the disco music always incorporates the latest sounds in town. Down: a mixture of rock music and over-the-top *sevillanas*.

SHOPPING

Semon (C D3)
→ *Carrer de Ganduxer, 31*
Tel. 93 201 65 08
Mon-Sat 10am–3pm, 5–9pm; Sun 10am–2pm
World-famous *traiteur-charcuteria*. In one corner is a tiny restaurant where you can try the goodies.

Foix de Sarrià (C C1)
→ *Carrer Major de Sarrià, 57 / Tel. 93 203 07 14*
Daily 8am–9pm
A hundred-year-old establishment offering specialties that never go out of fashion: *petxines*, shell-shaped chocolate-

covered almond cookies. Try the delicious home-made *horchata* (a drink made from *chufa* fruit), the ice creams and the mousses. Everything tastes great.

La Fuente (C D3)
→ *Carrer de Johann Sebastian Bach, 20*
Tel. 93 201 15 13
Mon-Fri 9am–2pm, 4.30–8.30pm; Sat 9am–2pm
A *bodega* (cellar-bar), spread over 1,076 sq ft where you can find 99% of the wines available on the Spanish market. Also a huge variety of liquors from all over the world.

Centros comerciales (C B3–D4)
Concentration of shopping centers along one section of the Avinguda Diagonal. Great for shopaholics, especially during the sales.

El Corte Inglés
→ *Avinguda Diagonal, 617*
Tel. 93 366 71 00
Practical store selling all the essentials.

Pedralbes Centre
→ *Avinguda Diagonal, 609*
Tel. 93 410 68 21
Chic, designer shopping.

L'Illa Diagonal
→ *Avinguda Diagonal, 545*
Tel. 93 444 00 00
Huge and cosmopolitan.

PLAÇA DELS PAÏSOS CATALANS

CAMP NOU

FINCA MIRALLES / STATUE OF GAUDÍ

Plaça del Dr
A DE LES CORTS
Plaça de
AVINGUDA DIAGONAL
AV. DE PAU CASALS
ENTENÇA
MATA
CARRER DE DEU
CARRER DE
AVINGUDA
AVINGUDA DE SARRIA
C. DE TENOR VIÑAS
C. DE BORI I FONTESTÀ
NUMÀNCIA
JARDINS DEL POETA E. MARQUINA
DE CALVET
C. DE LA CARAVEL·LA LA NIÑA
TEMPLE
Plaça de
St. Gregori
Taumaturg
C. DEL J.S. BACH
C. DE LES ESCOLES PIES
CARRER DE GANDUXER
CARRER DE LA REINA VICTORIA
C. DEL DR FLEMING
DEL
AVINGUDA DE LA RIBA
RONDA
CARRER DEL
III Plaça de Prat
de la Riba
PG. DE ST. JOAN BOSCO
CARRER ALT DE GIRONELLA
CARRER DE MODOLELL
AUGUSTA
LA BONANOVA
GENERAL MITRE
VIA
DOCTOR ROUX
COL·LEGI DE
LES TERESIANES
MIL ANSAT
C. DE VERGÓS
LES TRES TORRES
Plaça de Joaquim
Pena
Plaça
d'artos
CARRER DEL CARDENAL SENTMENAT
CARRER MAJOR DE SARRIÀ
FONTCOBERTA
C. DE GANDUXER
C. DEL DOCTOR CARULLA
DE CALATRAVA
CARRER PAU ALCOVER
CARRER DEL EMANCIPACIÓ
Plaça de
l'Orient
CARRER DELS VERGÓS
SARRIÀ
VIA AUGUSTA
C. DEL PEDRO DE LA CREU
LES DALMASES
CARRER DE DALMASES
PASSEIG DE LA BONANOVA
CARRER DE LES ESCOLES PIES PLANELLA
D'IRADIER
MARGENAT
C. DOLORS MONSERDA
VIA AUGUSTA
Pl. de Sarrià
LA REINA DE MONTCADA
DE RAMON MIQUEL I PLANAS
D'ANGLI
C. DELS PLANELLA

JARDINS DE L'ESPANYA INDUSTRIAL

PARC JOAN MIRÓ

esa in his construction is 1889 building, Gaudí ...ed that he was a fine ...itect of structure as well ... genius of form.

...nca Miralles (C B2-3)
*...sseig de Manuel
...a, 55–61*
...nt of an astonishing ...ic-covered outer wall, ...gned by Gaudí in 1901, ...ds a bronze statue ...g homage to the ...er himself.

...mp Nou (C A4)
*...rer Arístides Maillol, 12
3 496 36 08
...at 10am–6.30pm; Sun
...ublic hols 10am–2pm
...um)*
...lona's citizens love

their football... and they love Barça (FC Barcelona), proudly headquartered in the magnificent stadium of Camp Nou. This ancient rival to the Real Madrid team, 'the army of Catalonia' has become a symbol of the Catalan identity. The stadium, homeground to the players in *blaugrana* (blue and maroon), and one of the largest in Europe, was built in 1957. A museum traces the history of the club since 1889.

★ **Plaça dels Països Catalans (C** B5)
Laid out in 1983 by Viaplana and Piñon, architects of the superb CCCB building in El

Raval (see **B** ★), this avant-garde square has been the subject of a number of heated controversies. Spartan, open to the elements, and located at a crossover of roads and railway lines, it shows that even simple concrete and metal shelters can be appealing.

★ **Jardins de l'Espanya Industrial (C** B6)
→ *Plaça de Joan Peiro
Daily 10am–6pm (7pm
March and Oct; 8pm April
and Sep; 9pm May–Aug)*
A subtle dialogue between nature, contemporary art and modern architecture, this park, which backs on

to the station at Sants, is built on the site of a former textile factory. Unusual view over the sculptures from the top of the red-and-yellow striped lighthouses surrounding the lake.

★ **Parc Joan Miró (C** C6)
→ *Carrer de Tarragona
Daily 10am–6pm (7pm March
and Oct; 8pm April and Sep;
9pm May–Aug)*
The former slaughter-houses have now disappeared and in their place stands this park, created in the 1980s. The highlights here are the palm grove, the playgrounds, a pergola and Miró's *Bird Lady*.

MUSEU DE LA MÚSICA

LA PEDRERA

★ Park Güell (D D2)
→ *Carrer d'Olot*
Daily 10am–6pm (7pm March and Oct; 8pm April and Sep; 9pm May–Aug)
Originally planned to be a garden suburb, this incredible, bizarre and jubilant design is one of Gaudí's strokes of genius. Before moving on to the Sagrada Família, Gaudí lived here for 20 years, yet only the park itself and two of the houses were ever completed. Don't miss the Hall of a Hundred Columns (there are only 86), the staircase with its mosaic salamander, and the undulating bench by Jujol,

a follower of Gaudí.
**★ Avinguda
del Tibidabo (D** B1)
→ *By tram from Avinguda del Tibidabo Station to Plaça del Doctor Andreu*
Fri 11am–8pm; Sat, Sun and public hols 9am–9pm
Daily in summer
Two old blue trams *(tramvia blau)*, in service since 1902, run along this avenue lined with modern buildings. At the end are breathtakingly clear views over the city and the bay. Anyone who likes heights should take the funicular up to the fairground, where the views are even more breathtaking.

★ Casa Terrades (D C5)
→ *Av. Diagonal, 416–420*
The House of Spires (1903), with its six towers, has the air of a northern European castle. This masterpiece, by Puig i Cadafalch, is strongly influenced by Gothic architecture.
**★ Museu
de la Música (D** B5)
→ *Avinguda Diagonal, 373*
Tel. 93 416 11 57
Tue, Thu–Sun 10am–2pm, Wed 10am–8pm
Inspired by the spatial arrangement and layout used in Gothic architecture, the Museum of Music (1902) is built around a central patio.

The building is as richly decorated inside as out. Major collection of guita
★ La Pedrera (D B6)
→ *Passeig de Gràcia, 92*
Tel. 93 484 59 95
Daily 10am–8pm (midni Fri–Sat in summer)
All undulations, hollow and humps, the façade La Pedrera (literally 'Th Quarry') resembles a c eroded by years of sea wind. Gaudí designed five-story building at th height of his career in fashioning the materia and giving form to his extraordinary, overflo fantasy in everything f the underground car p

D

CASA TERRADES

PARK GÜELL

AVINGUDA DEL TIBIDABO

After the demolition of the fortified city walls in the 1850s, 'L'Eixample' (literally 'expansion'), was the result of a plan by engineer Ildefons Cerdà to come up with an egalitarian, rational program of town-planning. He built a democratic, grid-like district which links the old city with Gracià. Because of its many stunning Modernist designs it has become a favorite area for visitors with an interest in architecture. Gràcia, suburban and arty, is a dense web of streets and squares, combining traditional commercial activity with the avant-garde. The number of cafés, bars and restaurants here seems to increase almost daily.

EL JAPONÉS DEL TRAGALUZ FLASH FLASH

RESTAURANTS

Casa Amalia (**D** C6)
→ *Passatge Mercat, 4–6*
Tel. 93 458 94 58 / Tue-Sun (Mon-Fri in summer) 1–3.30pm, 9–10.45pm Closed first week in Aug
Located in a narrow passageway just next to the hustle and bustle of the covered market. The recently restored Casa Amalia serves up a breezy menu of delicious and freshly prepared dishes which vary according to the season, using the best produce that the Concepció market has to offer. Lunch menu 8.40 €.

El Japonés del Tragaluz (**D** B5)
→ *Passatge de la Concepció, 2*
Tel. 93 487 25 92
Daily 1.30–4pm, 8.30pm–midnight (1am Fri-Sat)
Japanese restaurant with Barcelona designer-décor: the extreme modernity is in complete harmony with the cuisine that prevails here. Tempura, sushi, rice and noodles dishes. Around 15 €.

Flash Flash (**D** B4)
→ *Carrer Granada del Penedès, 25*
Tel. 93 237 09 90
Daily 1pm–1.30am
The ultimate in tasty *tortillas* and pop art. Opened in the 1970s, this was once the hangout of the 'divine left' (a movement which united intellectuals and architects). Even today it is a great place to be seen. The hamburgers are worth trying.
À la carte 20 €.

Bilbao (**D** C5)
→ *Carrer del Perill, 33*
Tel. 93 458 96 24
Mon-Sat 1–4pm, 9–11pm Closed Aug
Classic restaurant which, for the past 45 years, has relied on serving unfussy, unpretentious, good-quality food using market-fresh produce. *Bacalao* (cod) specialties.
À la carte 35 €.

Tragaluz (**D** B5)
→ *Passatge de la Concepció, 5*
Tel. 93 487 06 21
Daily 1.30–4pm, 8.30pm–midnight
The stark designer setting is softened by the use of natural materials: wood and glass-diffused lighting. Traditional and faultless Catalan cuisine, lightened by a touch of creativity. Tempting tapas served sizzling in the Tragabar on the ground floor. À la carte 40 €.

DEL SOL

MOND CLUB (CIBELES)

VINÇON

La Balsa (north of **D** A1, off map)
→ *Carrer Infanta Isabel, 4*
Tel. 93 211 50 48
Mon 2–3.30pm; Tue-Sat
2–3.30pm, 9–11.30pm
Set in the heart of luxuriant greenery, this restaurant is a Barcelonese favorite. Imaginative and seasonal Catalan cuisine. In August, buffet dinner 25 €. À la carte 40 €.

CAFÉS, TAPAS

Molina Xarcuteria (**D** B3)
→ *Plaça Molina, 1*
Tel. 93 200 57 69
Mon-Sat 8am–10pm;
Sun 8am–3pm
Traditional *charcuteria*: the best *embutidos ibéricos* and Catalan specialties: *butifarra*, ham, *fuet*. Everything can be eaten in or taken out.
À la carte 13 €.

Bar París (**D** A5)
→ *Carrer de París, 187*
Tel. 93 209 85 30
Daily 7am–1am
Recently renovated, this 67-year-old bar continues to attract a young crowd who come here to fill up on the *raciones* (large-portioned tapas). Noisy and usually packed, it's a favorite place for a late snack or early breakfast.

Gimlet (**D** A4)
→ *Carrer Santaló, 46*
Tel. 93 201 53 06 / Daily
7pm–2.30am (3am Fri-Sat)
Two-thirds gin to one-third lime juice: the favorite cocktail of Philip Marlowe, Raymond Chandler's detective,
has given its name to this cozy bar, where bright young things come to be seen. The tapas at next-door's Casa Fernández are a safe bet for anyone in need of sustenance.

Plaça del Sol, Plaça de la Virreina
These squares are Gràcia's main attraction. Their terraces are always full to brimming: the cafés serve *bocadillos* (sandwiches), the perfect substitute for dinner after a movie at the nearby cinema, and they have a faithful following of customers who come here to mix and chat.

Café del Sol (**D** B4)
→ *Plaça del Sol, 16*
Tel. 93 415 56 63
Daily 1pm–0.30am
Good tapas (cockles and anchovies in sauces) and a sunny terrace.

Virreina (**D** C4)
→ *Plaça de la Virreina, 1*
Tel. 93 237 98 80
Daily 10am–2am
Delicious sandwiches.

NIGHTCLUBS

Mond Bar (**D** B4)
→ *Plaça del Sol, 21*
Tel. 93 457 38 77
Daily 8.30pm–6am
Soft lighting, comfortable sofas, trip-hop and techno music. Every night influential DJs preside, with music accompanied by slide shows. Come Friday, the club moves to an old-style ballroom, Mond Club (at Carrer Còrsega 363 (**D** C5), 0.30–6am). Unmissable.

El Universal (**D** A4)
→ *Carrer de Marià Cubí, 184 / Tel. 93 201 35 96*
Mon-Thu 11pm–3am
(5am Fri-Sat)
'In' place, full of beautiful people sporting the latest fashions. Set on two levels with house music downstairs and a cozy salon upstairs. Good place to talk and dance.

SHOPPING

Vinçon (**D** B6)
→ *Passeig de Gràcia, 96*
Tel. 93 215 60 50 / Mon-Sat
10am–2pm, 4.30–8.30pm
The latest designs in household items and furniture, spread over 3,500 sq yards.

Quílez (**D** B6)
→ *Rambla de Catalunya, 63*

Tel. 93 215 23 56
Mon-Fri 9am–2pm, 4.30–8.30pm; Sat 9am–2pm
Stunning window display with hundreds of different preserves: cockles, mussels, anchovies. Inside, a huge range of beers, wines and liquors.

Mauri (**D** B6)
→ *Rambla de Catalunya, 102 / Tel. 93 215 10 20*
Mon-Sat 8am–9pm;
Sun 9am–3pm
Delicious pastries and croissants.

Camper (**D** B6)
→ *Rambla de Catalunya, 122 Tel. 93 217 23 84*
Mon-Sat 10am–9pm
Very comfortable, hard-wearing shoes (with increasingly trendy designs as well), and attractive shops seem to be the recipe for the incredible success this Majorcan shoe brand has enjoyed across Europe for the past few years.

Dom (**D** B6)
→ *Passeig de Gràcia, 76*
Tel. 93 487 11 81
Mon-Sat 10.30am–8.30pm
9pm Sat)
If Dom didn't exist, movie maker Pedro Almodóvar would have invented it. The tone is low-budget pop and kitsch – useful presents and utterly useless gadgets.

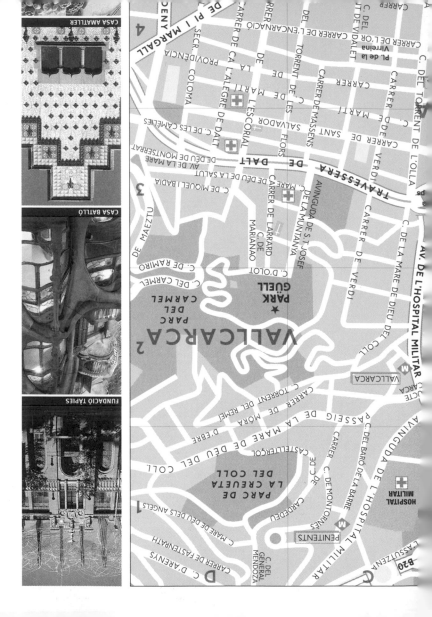

CASA AMATLLER

CASA BATLLÓ

FUNDACIÓ TÀPIES

VALLCARCA 2

PARC
DEL
CARMEL

PARC DE
LA CREUETA
DEL COLL

PARC DE
LA CREUETA
DEL COLL 1

PARK
GÜELL
★

HOSPITAL
MILITAR

AV. DE L'HOSPITAL MILITAR

AV. DE L'HOSPITAL MILITAR

VALLCARCA

PENITENTS

C. DE PI I MARGALL

C. DEL TORRENT DE L'OLLA

CARRER DE L'ENCARNACIÓ

CARRER DE L'OR

CARRER DE VIDALET

Pl. de la
Virreina

PROVIDÈNCIA

SECR. COLOMA

DE LA MARE DE DÉU DE MONTSERRAT

TORRENT DE LES FLORS

CARRER DE MARTÍ

CARRER DE MARTÍ

TORRENT DE L'ESCORIAL

C. DE LES CAMÈLIES

C. DE L'ALEGRE DE DALT

CARRER DE MASSENS

SANT SALVADOR

AV. DE LA MARE DE DÉU DE LA SALUT

CARRER DE DALT

TRAVESSERA DE DALT

C. DE VERDI

CARRER DE VERDI

CARRER DE VERDI

C. DE LA MARE DE DÉU DEL COLL

C. DE MIQUEL I BADIA

DE MAEZTU

DE RAMIRO

C. DEL CARMEL

C. D'OLOT

AVINGUDA DE S.T JOSEF DE LA MUNTANYA

CARRER DE LARRARD

C. DE MARIANAO

C. DE

CARRER DE MORA D'EBRE

C. TORRENT DEL REMEI

PASSEIG DE LA MARE DE DÉU DEL COLL

C. DE CASTELLTERÇOL

CARRER DE MONTORNÈS

C. DEL BARÓ DE LA BARRE

C. DE LA BARRE

C. DE MARE DE DÉU DELS ÀNGELS

CARRER DE FASTENRATH

C. D'ARENYS

C. DEL GENERAL MENDOZA

CARDEDEU

AVINGUDA DE L'HOSPITAL MILITAR

L'ASSUTZENA

B20

CARRER DE BRUNIQUER
CARREK
C. DE SAR
TAXDIRT
DE TEROL
JOANIC
ERA DE GRÀCIA
TRAVESSERA DE GRÀCIA
CARRER DE TORDERA
C. JOAN DE SANT NÀPOLS ANTONI MARIA CLARET
C. TORRES
DEL PERILL
CARRER DE LA INDÚSTRIA 5
LA SAGRADA FAMÍLIA
ER DE CÒRSEGA
CARRER DE CÒRSEGA
C. DEL ROSSELLÓ
DEL ROSSELLÓ
SAGRADA FAMÍLIA
AVINGUDA DIAGONAL
VERDAGUER
CARRER DE PROVENÇA
Pl. de la Sagrada Família
MALLORCA
Pl. Mossèn Jacint Verdaguer
MALLORCA SAGRADA FAMÍLIA
E VALÈNCIA
C. DE VALÈNCIA 6
AVINGUDA DIAGONAL
AGÓ
CARRER D'ARAGÓ
SELL DE C CENT
C. DEL CONSELL D DE CENT

CASA LLEÓ MORERA

SAGRADA FAMÍLIA

Map F →

pe's first) to the
al chimneys on top.
grada Família (**D** D6)
rrer Mallorca, 401
3 208 04 14 / Daily
6pm (8pm in summer)
, in 1886, the 31-year-
audí accepted the
ission to design a
othic religious
ng, he certainly was
vare that this project
be a life's work. He
nere for 16 years,
t as a recluse,
ng in the crypt. Still
shed and even today
use of great
versy, the
uction of this
ral is a drama that

continues to unfold. Two of
the three façades are now
visible: that of the much-
criticized 'Passion' was
completed in 1986 by the
artist Subirachs.
★ Casa Lleó Morera (**D** B6)
→ *Passeig de Gràcia, 35*
The most sober of the three
symbolic buildings that
make up the 'block of
discord' (Batlló, Amatller
and Morera). The lobby and
its Modernist staircase are
well worth seeing.
★ Casa Amatller (**D** B6)
→ *Passeig de Gràcia, 41*
Tel. 93 488 01 39 / Mon-Sat
10am–7pm (2pm Sun)
Another example of Puig i
Cadafalch's ability to draw

on the Gothic style and yet
break with uniformity and
the geometric rigor of the
Eixample. The façade is
that of a medieval palace
directly imported from
a Hanseatic city.
★ Fundació Tàpies (**D** B6)
→ *Carrer d'Aragó, 255*
Tel. 93 487 03 15
Tue-Sun 10am 8pm
This splendid building, the
first example of Modernist
architecture (1879), and
originally a publishing
house, gave Domènech i
Montaner an opportunity
to put into practice his
principles of rationalist
construction, while drawing
on a neo-Mudejar style.

Today the building is topped
by a wire sculpture by
Tàpies. The foundation
houses the most complete
collection of the artist's
work, as well as a library.
★ Casa Batlló (**D** B6)
→ *Passeig de Gràcia, 43*
Fabulous creation by Gaudí
(1904); the roof resembles a
giant's spine while the base
of the columns are
reminiscent of enormous
elephant's feet. Twinkling
and colorful, covered in tiny
pieces of mosaic, the
façade appears as if it is
covered in fish scales. It is
really worth passing by
again at night when the
façade is illuminated.

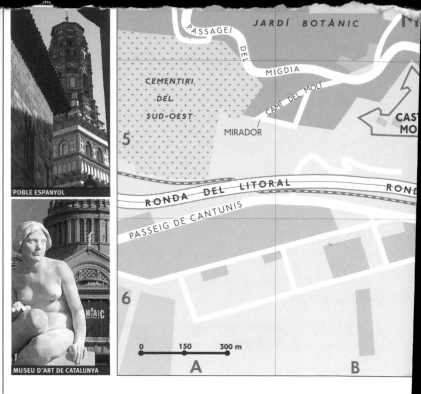

POBLE ESPANYOL

MUSEU D'ART DE CATALUNYA

★ Fundació La Caixa (E B2)
→ *Avinguda del Marquès de Comillas, 6*
Tel. 93 476 8600
Tue-Sat 11am–8pm
There are no external clues as to the wealth, creativity and imagination that lurks behind these thick red-brick walls. The former Casarramona textile mill, designed by Puig i Cada-falch in 1913, now houses an Arts Center. One room was opened during the FC Barça exhibition and the whole building has come into operation in July 2001.
★ Font Màgica (E B2)
→ *Avinguda de la Reina Maria Cristina*

Oct-April: Fri-Sat 7–9pm; May-Sep 8pm–midnight
A gigantic fountain built for the Universal Exhibition in 1929, the spectacle of the changing water jets and the light and sound shows impressed the entire world. Restored in the 1950s, it is still one of the most amazing sights in the city: the music of both *Abba* and Tchaikovsky has been used to accompany the dancing jets of water.
★ Pavelló Mies van der Rohe (E B3)
→ *Avinguda del Marquès de Comillas / Tel. 93 423 40 16*
Daily 10am–8pm
Bookstore: daily 10am–7pm

The first superb example of Modernist architecture in Barcelona, the German pavilion at the Universal Exhibition of 1929 was designed by the leader of the Bauhaus movement. Demolished at the end of the event, this masterpiece was later reconstructed on the same spot (1986).
★ Poble Espanyol (E B3)
→ *Avinguda del Marquès de Comillas*
Tel. 93 325 78 66
Mon 9am–8pm; Tue-Thu 9am–2am; Fri-Sat 9am–4am; Sun 9am–midnight
Entering into Poble Espanyol is like seeing the whole of Spain in one go,

with the entire range of architectural styles from the different regions represented. Entrance to the village is via the ramparts of Avila; the Castillian plaza leads to Andalusian church and several typical Aragon houses. Touristy and ra artificial, although the shops have a certain charm. Very lively nigh
★ Museu Nacional de Catalunya (E B3)
→ *Palau Nacional, Parc de Montjuïc*
Tel. 93 622 03 75
Tue-Sat 10am–7pm (2.3 Sun and public hols)
One of the most beau

E

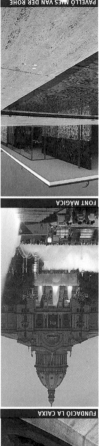

Map C →

Montjuïc / Poble Sec / Sant Antoni

A city of hills, Barcelona designated Montjuïc (easily visible from Barcelona's harborside) to be the center of the 1992 Olympic Games. The infrastructure was developed by a team of the most brilliant designers and today it is still the venue for major sports and leisure events, with superb walks along the coast. Poble Sec, at the foot of the hill, is the city's old theater area... A *moulin rouge* (now closed) is reminiscent of Paris' Pigalle, though the atmosphere here is now Bohemian rather than seedy. At Sant Antoni, bordering El Raval, shops and restaurants line the peaceful streets of this once working-class district.

CA L'ISIDRE   SIRVENT

RESTAURANTS

Quimet & Quimet (E D4)
→ Carrer de Poeta Cabanyes, 25
Tel. 93 442 31 42
Tue-Sat noon–4pm, 7–10.30pm; Sun noon–4pm. Closed Aug
Narrow *bodega* with walls lined with superb wines and serving delicious tapas: cod with tomatoes, tuna, Asturian cheese with chestnuts... Enjoy! Let the staff help you choose. Expect to pay around 13 €.

Dionisos (E D2)
→ Carrer de Comte d'Urgell, 90 / Tel. 93 451 54 17
Daily 1.30–4pm, 8.30pm–midnight
Greek specialties in a friendly, seaside-colored setting. Good food and background music in both the bar-*bodega* and restaurant. Set lunch menu 8 €. À la carte 18 €.

Restaurant de la Fundació Miró (E C4)
→ Parc de Montjuïc
Tel. 93 329 07 68
Tue-Sat 1–4pm
Luminous dining room thanks to large bay windows giving onto the park and the huge terrace. The cooking is excellent and the place highly recommended after a visit of the park. À la carte 18 €.

Elche (E D4)
→ Carrer de Vila i Vilà, 71
Tel. 93 441 30 89
Daily 1–5pm, 8pm–midnight
Named after a town situated several miles from Alicante, this place serves paellas made using traditional recipes. Very friendly place. À la carte 24 €.

Marisqueiro Panduriño (E D2)
→ Carrer Floridablanca, 3
Tel. 93 325 70 16
Tue-Sun 1–4pm, 8pm–midnight
Small and welcoming, this restaurant offers Galician specialties. Mostly seafood and fish dishes, but some typical inland dishes too. À la carte 30 €.

San Telmo (E D4)
→ Carrer de Vila i Vilà, 53
Tel. 93 441 30 78
Tue-Sat 1–4pm, 9–midnight
The right place to experience the Bohemian atmosphere which used to prevail when the theaters in this area thrived; Catalan specialties are served in a garden – the perfect setting. À la carte 30 €.

Ca l'Isidre (E D4)
→ Carrer Flors, 12
Tel. 93 441 11 39

TA ROJA

LA TERRAZZA

MERCAT DE SANT ANTONI

Mon-Sat 1.30–3.30pm,
8.30–11pm
Tucked away between
Raval and the Paralel
district, this restaurant
is easy to miss. Those in
the know, however, (one
of whom is said to be the
King of Spain himself) are
familiar with Ca l'Isidre's
delicious Catalan fare.
The daily menu is highly
recommended.
À la carte 60 €.

CAFÉS

Sirvent (**E** D3)
➜ *Carrer del Parlament, 56*
Tel. 93 441 27 20
Daily 8.30am–1am
(closed Jan-Feb)
Most Barcelonese claim
that for the past 85 years
this café has served the
finest *horchata* (a milky
drink made from the
almond-like *chufa* fruit),
and we believe them.
The ice cream and nougat
which is served here are
also delicious.

La Confiteria (**E** D4)
➜ *Carrer de Sant Pau, 128*
(going east, off map, at the
corner of Ronda de St Pau)
Tel. 93 443 04 58
Mon–Sat 7pm–3am
(midnight Sun)
Until the early 20th
century this building was
used by a pastrymaker

and has only recently
been converted into a bar.
During the day, locals sit
and chat over a coffee.
In the evening, the place
transforms itself into a
lively bar where actors,
stage crew and audience
alike come for an after-
show drink.

BARS, CABARET, NIGHTCLUBS

Los Juanele (**E** D3)
➜ *Carrer Aldana, 4*
Tel. 93 454 06 19
Thu-Sat 10pm–5.30am
Start with some tapas and
a glass or two of wine
before making for the
dance floor to dance the
sevillanas. Gypsies and
novices alike come here
and, on Thursday
evenings, there are dance
classes from 9–10pm.

Tinta Roja (**E** C3)
➜ *Carrer Creu dels*
Molers, 17
Tel. 93 443 32 43
Wed-Thu 8pm–1am (3am
Fri-Sat); shows Fri and Sat
One of Barcelona's
fairytale establishments.
A long way from designer
décor or electronic music,
this is a traditional-style
club. People come to soak
up the atmosphere of this
long-standing Argentinian
cabaret club. Don't miss

the tango displays at the
weekend.

Rouge (**E** D4)
➜ *Carrer de Poeta*
Cabanyes, 21
Tel. 93 442 49 85
Thu-Sat 11pm–3.30am
With the look of a private
club, this bar is one of
the most elegant in the
district, but it is also
slightly surreal: ring the
bell, enter, and cross the
well-lit lobby with its red
walls and comfortable
sofas, on which mostly
beautiful people languidly
rest. Expensive cocktails,
soul, jazz and lounge
music. Beware: on
Sunday afternoons the
place becomes a meeting
place for football
supporters!

La Terrazza (**E** B2)
➜ *Avinguda del Marquès*
de Comillas, Poble Espanyol
Tel. 93 272 49 80
Thu-Sat midnight–6am
Surrounded by pine trees,
this is the best place to
hear house music in
Barcelona. Shake your
stuff in the open air in
summer, next door in
winter. Drag queens,
gogo dancers and bunny
girls in abundance.

Mau Mau (**E** D4)
➜ *Carrer d'En*
Fontodrona 33
Tel. 60 686 06 17

Thu 11pm–2.30am (3am
Fri-Sat); Sun 7–11pm
DJs play funk, soul or
house music in this very
friendly, laid-back bar,
where a mainly young
and mainly local clientele
comes to relax.

**Club Apolo /
Nitsaclub** (**E** D4)
➜ *Carrer Nou de la*
Rambla, 113
Tel. 93 441 40 01
Fri-Sat 0.30–6am
Former ballroom, now a
key venue for electronic
music in Barcelona.

SHOPPING

**Mercat
de Sant Antoni** (**E** D3)
➜ *Carrer del Comte d'Urgell,*
1 / Tel. 93 423 42 87
Mon-Sat 7.30am–1.30pm,
5.30pm–8pm;
Sun 9am–2pm (books)
Some say this market,
laid out in the shape of
a Greek cross, and built
from metal and glass,
is the most authentic
building of its kind on Las
Ramblas. Its iron shutters
open onto colorful shops
selling fresh produce. On
Sundays book, coin and
music collectors take over.
Right opposite is the
terrace of the Els Tres café,
an ideal spot for a well-
earned break.

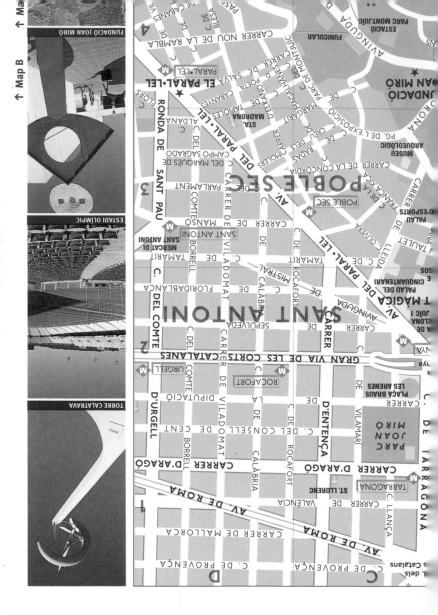

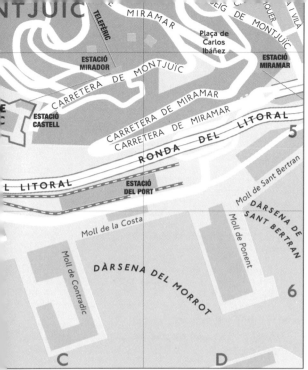

CASTELL DE MONTJUÏC

EL PARAL.LEL

ieval art museums in world. The principle ing of the 1929 ullion now contains ordinary collections man and Gothic art, notably frescos and shelves.

stell
ontjuïc (E B5)
rc de Montjuic
3 329 86 13
un 9.30am–8pm
a symbol of the ssion of the people, stle has stood on this r centuries. Today it es a military museum a stunning collection ient weapons, maps odels). Magnificent

views over the city from the castle ramparts.

★ El Paral.lel (E D4)
→ *Around Avinguda del Paral.lel*
The theaters, cabarets and music halls have all gone in this area, which, until the 1950s, resembled Paris's Montmartre. Only the huge chimneys remain of what was the central electricity power station, now a park popular with rollerbladers.

★ Fundació
Joan Miró (E C4)
→ *Parc de Montjuïc*
Tel. 93 329 19 08
Tue-Wed, Fri-Sat 10am–7pm
(8pm summer); Thu 10am–
9.30pm; Sun 10am–2.30pm

Miró was over 80 when the foundation that bears his name opened in 1975. Superbly organized, it contains the best of the work of the Catalan master, including his enormous bright tapestries, pencil drawings, sculptures and the colorful, childlike paintings for which he is best remembered.

★ Estadi Olímpic (E B4)**/**
i Palau Sant Jordi (E A4)
→ *Passeig Olímpic, 5–7 and 17–19 / Tel. 93 426 20 89*
Housing some 55,000 spectators in the stadium and 17,000 in the sports pavilion, the spectacular infrastructures built to

house the 1992 Olympic Games still host the city's major events. Designed by the Japanese architect Arata Isozaki, it is seen as a symbol of the modernity of the new Montjuïc district.

★ Torre Calatrava (E A3)
→ *Plaça Europa*
Easily identifiable from a distance, due to its unusual shape, the telecommunication tower was designed by the architect Caltrava in 1992. It is also constructed to work as a sundial, the spire's shadow being thrown onto its circular base, which is graduated to indicate the hour of the day.

GREENHOUSE (LA CIUTADELLA)

MUSEU DE ZOOLOGIA

AV. MARQUÈS DE L'ARGENTERA

ESTACIÓ DE FRANÇA

🅼 BARCELONETA

MUSEU D'ART MODERN

UNIVERSITAT POMPEU FABRA

PARC ZOOLÒGIC AQUARAMA

CARRER

CARRER

PARC CARLES I

CARRER DEL DOCTOR AIGUADER

RONDA DEL LITORAL

CIUTADELLA VILA OLÍMPICA 🅼

CARRER

C. DE BALBOA

CARRER DEL DOCTOR AIGUADER

PARC DE LES CASCADES

Pl. dels Voluntaris Olímpics

LA BARCELONETA

CARRER D'ANDREA DÒRIA

PARC DE LA BARCELONETA

HOSPITAL DEL MAR ✚

BARCELONETA

PASSEIG MARÍTIM DE LA BARCELONETA

Platja de la Barceloneta

0   150   300 m

A   B

★ Teatre nacional de Catalunya i l'Auditori (F C3)

→ *Corner of Plaça de les Arts and Carrer Lepant, 150 Tel. 93 306 57 00 (theater), 93 247 93 00 (auditorium)*
In 1997 Ricardo Bofill designed a theater whose grandiose silhouette was reminiscent of the Parthenon. The auditorium next door was opened in 1999: Madrilène Moneo was the designer of this new building with its state-of-the-art technology and extraordinary acoustics. The recent renovation of the district around the Plaça de les Glòries

Catalanes completes, some 150 years later, the original vision of Cerdà, who saw it as the city's new center.

★ Parc del Estació del Nord (F B3)

→ *Avinguda de Vilanova Daily 10am–6pm (7pm March and Oct; 8pm April and Sep; 9pm May–Aug)*
The most unusual park in Barcelona opened in 1988 behind the disused North Station. The sculptures by Beverly Pepper, in blue and white mosaic, are inspired by Gaudí. Strewn around the lawns, they brighten the park here and there, appearing by benches and behind trees.

★ Arc del Triomf (F A3)

→ *Passeig de Lluís Companys*
In 1888, the architect Vilaseca was asked to design a landmark that would symbolize the Universal Exhibition. He decided upon the classical theme of a triumphant arch and built the monumental arch using simple brick, to reflect the fashion at the time for neo-Mudéjar style.

★ Museus i zoo del Parc de la Ciutadella (F A4)

→ *Corner of Passeig de Pujades/Passeig de Picasso Tel. 93 225 67 80*
For a short cultural stopover, visit the Citadel park. Here you are spoilt

for choice: geological museum, zoological museum, modern Cata[?] art gallery, two green-houses and a zoo (wh[?] has as its mascot an a[?] gorilla answering to th[?] name of 'Snowflake'). All of these are house[?] either in splendid pav[?] from the 1888 Interna[?] Exhibition or former military buildings.

★ Parc de la Ciutadella (F [?]

→ *Corner of Passeig d[?] Pujades/Passeig de P[?] Daily 10am–6pm (7pm March and Oct; 8pm A[?] and Sep; 9pm May–A[?]*
Once the site of the [?]

F

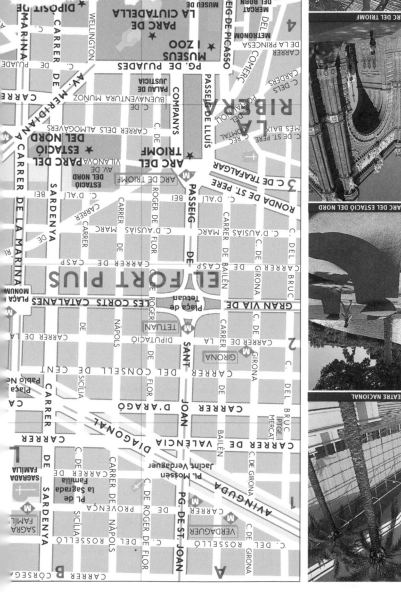

ARC DEL TRIOMF

PARC DEL ESTACIÓ DEL NORD

TEATRE NACIONAL

Even the people of Barcelona seem scarcely able to believe that before 1992 the coastal area of the city was nothing but a vast wasteland. Today it is a mystery how the city ever survived without its beaches, new parks and shopping centers filled with restaurants, bars and trendy nightclubs. Functional and modern, the transformations have resulted in the revival of the Poblenou area; the former factories have been turned into artists' studios, and the lively nightlife is in full swing seven nights a week. The Dreta area, more residential in tone, is worth a detour, if only for its markets.

ELS POLLOS DE LLULL   AGUA

RESTAURANTS

El Vaso de Oro (**F** A5)
→ *Carrer de Balboa, 6*
Tel. 93 319 30 98
Daily 9am–midnight
This small place is almost always busy, mostly packed with locals, who adore the tapas and dishes of the day served here. Excellent Catalan beer too. À la carte 10 €.

Els Pollos de Llull (**F** C4)
→ *Carrer de Ramón Turro, 13*
Tel. 93 221 32 06
Daily 1pm–1am
Following its success in a former warehouse a few streets away, this restaurant has relocated; it is almost identical to its former incarnation, only in a more comfortable space. What made the place a success has not changed: excellent grilled chicken and salads at reasonable prices (weekday lunch menu 5 €). Lively atmosphere. À la carte 12 €.

Espai Sucre (**F** A4)
→ *Carrer de la Princesa, 53*
Tel. 93 268 16 30
Tue-Sat 9–11pm
For those with a very sweet tooth, here is a restaurant that only cooks puddings (well, nearly: there are some savory dishes too). There are two menus, each with three or five dishes and a marked crescendo in the sugar content. The variety of flavors is absolutely amazing and the delicately constructed desserts are delicious. You can accompany each dish with a different wine, recommended by the chef (2 € per glass). The place is strange enough, perhaps, to be worth a visit. Menus at 21 € and 32 €.

San Fermín, la Sidrería de Barcelona (**F** C6)
→ *Moll de Gregal, 22 (Port Olímpic)*
Tel. 93 221 02 09
Tue-Sat 1–1am (4pm Sun)
If, despite (or perhaps because of) the dozens of restaurants squeezed along the quayside of Port Olímpic, you can't decide where to go for a good night out, this Basque cider-works is a safe bet. Good tapas, grilled meat and sausages, unlimited cider. À la carte 30 €.

Agua (**F** B5)
→ *Passeig Marítim de la Barceloneta, 30*
Tel. 93 225 12 72
Daily 1.30–4pm, 8.30pm–midnight (1am Fri-Sat)
A few yards from the extremely modern Port

ELS ENCANTS VELLS

IMAGINARIUM

Olímpic, this colonial-style restaurant opens right onto the beach. Delicious fish and seafood dishes, and a maritime atmosphere, of course. À la carte 35 €.

Xiringuito Escribà (F D5)
→ *Ronda del litoral, 42*
Tel. 93 221 07 29
Tue-Sun 10am–4pm
Xiringuito means 'greasy spoon', an odd name for this establishment which is far from being a run-down café. Run by the Escribà family, renowned confectioners and pastry-chefs, the place offers delicious fish specials, good tapas and salads, and a seaside terrace.
À la carte 35 €.

CAFÉS, TAPAS

El Tío Ché (F D4)
→ *Rambla del Poblenou, 44-46*
Tel. 93 309 18 72
Summer: daily 10am–1am (2am Fri-Sat). Winter: Thu-Tue 10am–1pm, 5–10pm
On Barcelona's other main boulevard, where the city still has the feel of a market town, food-lovers meet up at 'Uncle Ché' to drink a *granizado* or a *horchata*, eat an ice

cream or nibble some home-made nougat.

BARS, NIGHTCLUBS

Casino L'Aliança (F D4)
→ *Rambla del Poblenou, 42 / Tel. 93 225 28 14 (ring for the door man)*
Keep an eye on the varied program of this former theater: its list of performers is likely to include anything from Destiny's Child to the local brass band. It also rents out space for special events.

Razzmatazz (F C3)
→ *Carrer Almogàvers, 122*
Tel. 93 320 82 00/ 93 272 09 10 (clubs)
Fri-Sat 1–5am
Razzmatazz is an old concert hall that has been converted into a huge space dedicated to alternative culture: concerts, exhibitions, fashion shows... At the weekend that space is divided into a series of clubs that will delight music aficionados: for example there's indie pop rock at the Razz Club, pop and 60s at the Pop Bar, gothic at the Temple Beat, house and electro at the Loft. The coolest live music venue in town.

Suborn (F A4)
→ *Carrer de la Ribera, 18*
Tel. 93 310 11 10
Summer: Tue-Sun 11am–4am
Winter: Thu-Sat 8.30pm–4am
A former local bar, this has been transformed into a club where you can lunch (dishes prepared using market produce, 12 €), dine (a more imaginative menu) and enjoy sessions of techno music. Pleasant terrace under the arches of Passeig Picasso.

L'Ovella Negra (F B5)
→ *Carrer Zamora, 78*
Tel. 93 309 59 38 / Fri-Sat 5pm–3.30am (10pm Sun)
A bar with long wooden tables and a lively ambience – the ideal spot to drink a beer or sangria in the early part of the night.

Port Olímpic (F B-C5)
A touristic but very animated place at night. You will find that numerous nightclubs let you in for free, so hop in and out until you find what you're looking for: salsa, techno, pop...

Baja Beach Club
→ *Pg. Marítim de la Barceloneta, 34*
Tel. 93 225 91 00

SHOPPING

Els encants Vells: flea market (F C2)
→ *Carrer del Dos de Maig, 186 / Tel. 93 246 30 30*
Mon, Wed, Fri and Sat 9am–6pm
Venture here for an amazing range of bric-à-brac, with rumba music playing in the background. It's a little confusing, with the most surprising items seeming to appear out of nowhere just when you least expect them. To give you a head start: hats, dress-jewelry and other baubles on stand 15; 1960s furniture on stands 103–104; 1970s fashionwear on stands 106–111 and psychedelic colors and retro clothing on stands 112–120.

Imaginarium (F B5)
→ *Marina Village, Port Olímpic*
Tel. 93 221 52 57
Daily noon–8pm
Toy heaven for kids up to 10 years old.

Mango Outlet (F A2)
→ *Carrer de Girona, 37*
Tel. 93 412 29 35
Mon-Sat 10.15pm–9pm
Last years' collections by the Spanish brand Mango at incredible prices (between 20 and 50% discount).

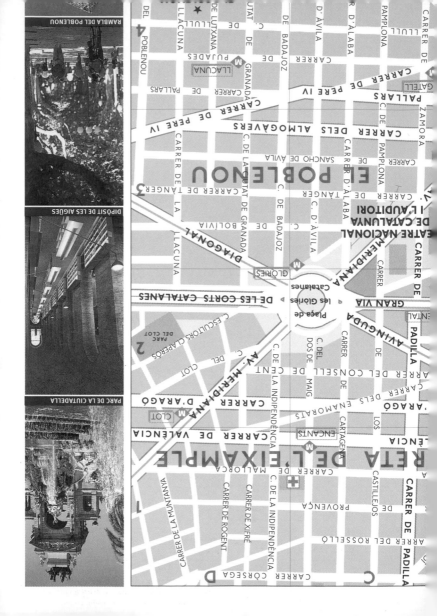

RAMBLA DEL POBLENOU

DIPÒSIT DE LES AIGÜES

PARC DE LA CIUTADELLA

CARRER DE LLULL

DE LUXANA
LLACUNA
DE POBLENOU
C. DE LLULL
UTAT
DE
DE BADAJOZ
D'ÀVILA
D'ÀLABA
PAMPLONA
CARRER DE LLULL

CARRER DE PERE IV
LLACUNA
DE GRANADA
CARRER DE PUJADES
PALLARS
CARRER DE PALLARS
GATELL
ZAMORA
C. DE PALLARS

CARRER DE PERE IV
CARRER DELS ALMOGÀVERS
SANCHO DE ÀVILA
CARRER DE PAMPLONA
CARRER D'ÀLABA

EL POBLENOU
CARRER DE TÀNGER
DE LA CIUTAT DE GRANADA
DE BADAJOZ
DE BOLÍVIA
C. D'ÀVILA
C. DE TÀNGER
CARRER DE TÀNGER

TEATRE NACIONAL
DE CATALUNYA
I L'AUDITORI

CARRER DE
CARRER DE

DIAGONAL
LLACUNA
GLÒRIES
CARRER DE PERE IV

DE LES CORTS CATALANES
Plaça de
les Glòries
Catalanes
GRAN VIA

AVINGUDA

PADILLA

MERIDIANA

PARC
DEL CLOT
C. ESCULTORS CLAPERÓS

DEL CLOT
C. DEL
CARRER DEL CONSELL DE CENT
C. DE DOS DE MAIG
CARRER DE
C. DE LA INDEPENDÈNCIA
DE
CARRER DELS ENAMORATS

CARRER D'ARAGÓ
CLOT
AV. MERIDIANA

CARRER DE VALÈNCIA
ENCANTS
CARTAGENA
CASTILLEJOS
PROVENÇA
CARRER DE PADILLA

DRETA DE L'EIXAMPLE

CARRER DE LA MUNTANYA
CARRER DE ROGENT
CARRER DE XIFRÉ
C. DE LA INDEPENDÈNCIA
CARRER DE MALLORCA
CARRER DE CÒRSEGA
CARRER DEL ROSSELLÓ
ARRER DEL ROSSELLÓ

...national Exhibition, formerly a military ...del, this has become ...green lung of the city ...acres). It has a ...umental waterfall, ...e of Barcelona's best-...vn sculptures and a ...ing lake. A real oasis ...v from the bustle of the ...ity, it is particularly ...lar on Sundays.

pòsit
es Aigües (F B4)
...rrer de Ramon Trías ...as, 25
...3 542 17 09
...Fri 8am–1.30pm;
...un and public hols
...–9pm
...idden gem is well

worth the effort it takes to find it. Adjoining the Citadel park, the water tower (1888), unknown by the majority of tourists, has been magnificently restored and converted into a university library. Behind a somewhat insignificant red-brick façade is a staggering maze of 46 ft-tall pillars.
★ **El Poblenou (F** D4)
→ *Around La Rambla del Poblenou*
Once one of the poorer areas of the city, Poblenou has benefited from the seafront renovations for the 1992 Olympic games. This workers' district was

once known as the 'Catalan Manchester ', but is today home to many artists, who have transformed the old factory premises into exciting studios and workshops (open days take place in early June). Don't hesitate to climb the perpendicular streets to La Rambla del Poblenou, a thoroughfare planted to resemble Provinçal courtyards.
★ **Port Olímpic /**
Vila Olímpica (F C5)
→ *Bogatell subway station, then head for the sea*
This extraordinary example of urban redevelopment was led by architects Josep

Martorell, Oriol Bohigas and Englishman David Mackay. The reshaping of the old industrial seafront for the Olympic Games has given the city an area entirely devoted to sport and leisure. The Olympic village, built to accommo-date 15,000 competitors and support staff, has today been reconverted into a residential zone with 2,000 apartments. Where previously the dilapidated dockside buildings masked the view of the sea there are now some 2 ½ miles of beach, with restaurants, bars, and extraordinarily avant-garde architecture.

Hostal Fernando (B C4)
→ *Carrer de Ferran Puíg, 31*
Tel. 93 301 79 93
In one of the liveliest
streets in the old city. Not
particularly charming, but
the rooms are spotlessly
clean. From 55 €.

Hostal-Residencia
Oliva (B D1-2)
→ *Passeig de Gràcia, 32*
Tel. 93 488 01 62
In the heart of L'Eixample
in a stylish building
(delightful stairwell and
elevator), this well-kept
and equally stylish hotel
has large rooms, some
overlooking the Modernist
buildings on Passeig de
Gràcia. From 55 €.

Hostal Lausanne (B C3)
→ *Avinguda del Portal*
de l'Àngel, 24
Tel. 93 302 11 39
The Hostal Lausanne
has a beautiful entrance
decorated with *azulejos*
(glazed ceramic tiles). The
guesthouse on the first floor

is in the same colorful style:
the rooms themselves are
basic but well kept.
Convenient for Plaça de
Catalunya. 48–68 €.

Hostal Fontanella (B D3)
→ *Via Laietana, 71*
Tel. 93 317 59 43
Very clean and well kept.
Eleven rooms and a friendly,
attentive owner. From 58 €.

Hostal Palermo (B C4)
→ *Carrer de la Boqueria, 21*
Tel. 93 302 40 02
The old, red floor tiles give
away the incredible age of
this small hotel. Freshly
renovated, well-kept rooms.
59–75 €.

Hostal Eden (D A6)
→ *Carrer de Balmes, 55*
Tel. 93 454 73 63
Just a few yards from Gaudí
's Casa Batlló, this guesthouse, in a building dating
from the early 20th century,
has perfectly-equipped
rooms (with TV and
jacuzzis). Pleasant, quiet
and welcoming. From 60 €.

60 – 80 €

Hostal-Residencia
Ramos (B B4)
→ *Carrer de l'Hospital, 36*
Tel. 93 302 07 23
A guesthouse right on the
edge of El Raval and just
a few paces from Las
Ramblas. Peaceful rooms
overlooking the Sant Agustí
church square. From 65 to
69 €, room with balcony.

Hostal Plaza (B D3)
→ *Carrer Fontanella, 18*
Tel. 93 301 01 39
As kitsch as they come:
pink and blue rooms with
mirrors hanging over the
beds, photos of Marilyn
Monroe, sticks of incense
and a disco glitterball in
the entrance hall. Some
rooms have a view of the
cathedral. Very quiet.
From 67 €.

Hotel Peninsular (B B4)
→ *Carrer de Sant Pau, 34-6*
Tel. 93 302 31 38
One of the best addresses

under this category.
Orginally a Carmelite
monastery, this hotel's
main charm is that it is
laid out around a sunny
green and cream patio,
surrounded by balconies
leading to the guest room
From 70 €, with breakfast

Hostal Jardi (B C4)
→ *Plaça Sant Josep Oriol*
Tel. 93 301 59 00
One of the best
guesthouses for the price
ideally situated just
opposite the Santa Maria
del Pi basilica. Obviously
the rooms with a view of
the basilica are the best
but they tend to be a litt
on the noisy side.
From 80 €.

80 – 120 €

Hotel España (B B4)
→ *Carrer de Sant Pau, ç*
Tel. 93 318 17 58
For those who like
Modernist architecture:

AIRPORT

Aeroport del Prat
7 miles to the south of Barcelona
→ Tel. 93 298 38 38
Barcelona city center – Airport links
Aerobus shuttle
→ *6am–midnight, every 15 mins (40 mins). Ends Plaça Catalunya. Price: 3.45 €. The cheap and reliable option.*
By train
→ *Every 30 mins 5.43am–10.16pm (25 mins). Price: 2.20 €*
By taxi
→ *13–16 € with a 20% supplement after 10pm and at weekends (30–50 mins)*

AIRPORT

TRAINS & STATIONS

Estació de Sants
(**C** B5) National and international lines. Airport links.
Estació de França
(**A** E2) National and regional trains. Some European services.
Informations RENFE
→ *Tel. 90 224 02 02 or 93 490 11 22 (International) Daily 7.30am–10.30pm*

INTERNATIONAL

Estació Barcelona Nord (**D** B3)
→ *Carrer Ali Bei, 80 Tel. 93 265 65 08*

Except where otherwise indicated, the prices given are for a double room with en-suite bathroom. Hotel (7%) tax is not included. Reservations advised.

Less than 40 €

Alberg Kabul (**A** C1)
→ *Plaça Reial, 17 Tel. 93 318 51 90*
One of the most charming youth hostels in the city, overlooking Plaça Reial. Rooms with 4, 6 or 8 beds (ask for a room with a view over the square). No reservations: just turn up any time after 8am. 19 € / person.
Hostal Malda (**B** C4)
→ *Carrer del Pi, 5 Tel. 93 317 30 02*
These former elegant apartments have been turned into a busy guesthouse (it is always full so book ahead). The owner is very hospitable and

claims not to have raised his prices for years. Twenty-three rooms, two with en-suite bathrooms. The shared bathrooms are spotless. 24–25 €.
Hostal La Terrassa (**B** B4)
→ *Carrer de Junta de Comerç, 11 Tel. 93 302 51 74*
Tucked away in a quiet street close to Las Ramblas, this guesthouse has two points in its favor: reasonable rates and a charming terrace where you can eat breakfast. 36 € with bathroom, 30 € without.
Pensión Francia (**A** D1)
→ *Carrer Rera Palau, 4 (Pla de Palau) Tel. 93 319 03 76*
Large, well-kept guesthouse, ideal for visitors who want to be close to both La Barceloneta and the beaches. On top of that the pensión is also close to the El Born

district which is fast becoming trendy. 27 € for a room without bathroom (immaculate shared showers); 40–55 € for an en-suite bathroom.

40 – 60 €

Pensión Rondas (**B** E2)
→ *Carrer de Girona, 4 Tel. 93 232 51 02*
Nine rooms, all well looked after by a dynamic, helpful brother and sister duo. From 45–50 €.
Hostal Rembrandt (**B** C3)
→ *Carrer de Portaferrissa, 23 / Tel. 93 318 10 11*
Small rooms, but clean and reasonably attractive. Pleasant terrace where guests can meet. From 50 €.
Hostal-Residencia Barcelona (**E** D4)
→ *Carrer del Roser, 40 Tel. 93 443 27 06*
Set a little apart from the touristy turmoil of Las

Ramblas, this simple guesthouse is in the heart of the old theater district. Rooms are equipped with televisions and there is a communal refrigerator. From 51 €.
Hostal Benidorm (**A** B1)
→ *Rambla dels Caputxins 37 / Tel. 93 302 20 54*
You could not hope for more: this is the perfect location, right on Las Ramblas, with some quiet rooms overlooking the extraordinary chimneys of Gaudí's Palau Güell. Beautiful bathrooms. Efficient but somewhat hasty service. From 52 €.
Pensión Norma (**D** B4)
→ *Carrer Gran de Gràcia, 87 / Tel. 93 237 44 78*
A guesthouse which is usually quiet, even at the height of the tourist season. Modest rooms, but extremely light and therefore very pleasant. From 48 to 50 €.

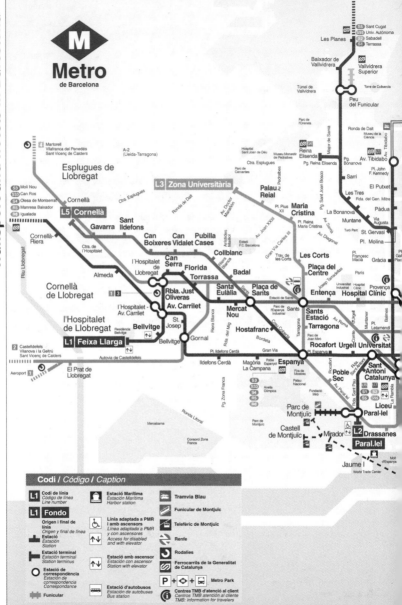

Transport and hotels in Barcelona

M Metro de Barcelona

Letters **(A, B...)** relate to the matching sections. Letters on their own refer to the spread with useful addresses. Letters followed by a star **(A★)** refer to the spread with the fold-out map and places to visit. The number **(1)** refers to the double page **Welcome to Barcelona!**

TAXIS

Recognizable by their yellow and black color. If the green light is on the taxi is available.

Fares
The basic rate (0.50€/mile) applies Mon–Fri 6am–10pm. Outside these times prices are subject to a 20% supplement.
➜ *Minimum charge 1.80 € plus the cost of the journey)*

Radio taxis
Barnataxi
➜ *Tel. 93 357 77 55*
Fono-Taxi
➜ *Tel. 93 300 11 00*

BY CAR

Documentation
EU and US drivers' licenses are recognized.

Speed limits
70 mph on freeways,
30 mph in built-up areas.

Alcohol levels
Limit 0.5 g/l.
Regular checks.

Parking
Street parking
Charges apply Mon-Sat 9am–2pm and 4–8pm (2 hours max).
➜ *1.70 € / hour*
Supervized parking
Marked by a white 'P' on a blue background. Strongly advised for vehicles with foreign license plates.
➜ *Around 1.60 €/ hour or pounds*
Plaça de los Glòries Catalanes
➜ *93 428 45 95*
The traffic officials are very vigilant, so beware. Protected areas are marked with orange signs.
To retrieve your vehicle, plus a fine.

MAIN THOROUGHFARES

this hotel was designed by Domènech i Montaner in 1902 (the ground floor is still superb). Rooms are a little disappointing though. From 86 €.

Hotel Urquinaona (**B** D2)
➜ *Ronda de Sant Pere, 24*
Tel. 93 268 13 36
Wonderful value for money. This former guesthouse has given way to a brand new hotel, with a sober, cool, minimalist décor. Rooms are comfortable and equipped as one would expect today, but ask for one giving onto the street (and on the upper floors), as those at the back give onto a wall. Excellent service. From 89 €.

Hotel Granvía (**B** CD2)
➜ *Gran Vía de les Corts Catalanes, 642*
Tel. 93 318 19 00
The decadent charm of this Modernist-style hotel has survived renovation. Here you can still eat in

the richly decorated dining room (complete with paintings and chandeliers). Modern rooms; from 110 €.

Hotel Metropol (**A** C1)
➜ *Carrer Ample, 31*
Tel. 93 310 51 00
Completely renovated ten years ago, the early 20th-century rooms overlook the strangely quiet street, close to the old port. From 110 €.

Hotel Mesón Castilla (**B** B2)
➜ *Carrer de Valldonzella, 5*
Tel. 93 318 21 82
Close to the Centre de Cultura Contemporània de Barcelona, in a street away from the activity of El Raval. A very comfortable hotel with quaint charm. From 117 € including breakfast.

Hotel Suizo (**A** D1)
➜ *Plaça de l'Àngel, 12*
Tel. 93 310 61 08
Very beautiful building located where the old Romanesque prisons once stood. The attic rooms are

especially adorable. From 122 €.

Hotel Rialto (**B** C4)
➜ *Carrer de Ferran, 42*
Tel. 93 318 52 12
Between Plaça Sant Jaume and Las Ramblas, this lovely hotel, birthplace of Joan Miró, has been magnificently restored. Unusual fossil collection in the restaurant. From 122 €.

Hotel Oriente (**A** B1)
➜ *Las Ramblas, 45–47*
Tel. 93 302 25 58
This hotel (1842), which claims to be the oldest in Barcelona, is situated in a Franciscan monastery. The cloister, which has been turned into a huge ballroom with a Catalan-style Art Nouveau décor (worth the detour), has entertained famous singers and great musicians who come to perform at the Liceu Opera House next door. Plain, comfortable, quiet rooms. From 131 €.

METRO

PUBLIC TRANSPORT

Different organizations run the public transport services in Barcelona:
TMB bus and metro
FGC internal and suburban railway service.

More than 120 €

Hotel Nouvel (**B** C3)
→ *Carrer de Santa Ana, 20*
Tel. 93 301 82 74
In a quiet street off Las Ramblas, close to Plaça de Catalunya, this tastefully decorated hotel still retains its Art Nouveau influence. Very comfortable rooms, one with jacuzzi. From 145 €.

Hotel Gaudí (**A** B1)
→ *Carrer Nou de la Rambla, 12 / Tel. 93 317 90 32*
Very well situated, almost opposite Palau Güell and close to Las Ramblas. The design of the entrance hall imitates the Gaudí hallmarks (colors and mosaics), but the rooms themselves are classic in style. From 150 €.

Hotel Colón (**B** D4)
→ *Av de la Catedral, 7*
Tel. 93 301 14 04
www.hotelcolon.es
From the top floor of the hotel you enjoy a stunning view of the cathedral: an equally good vantage point for the *sardana* dance displays which take place outside the cathedral on Sunday mornings. Terraces, cozy rooms and attentive service (220 € the double room). Under the same management is the nearby Regencia Colón: similar in quality but less expensive (from 145 €).

Hotel Duques de Bergara (**B** C2)
→ *Carrer de Bergara, 11*
Tel. 93 301 51 51
A 1898 Modernist marvel with ornate glass roof and marble staircase that should not leave you feeling indifferent. The building first opened as a luxurious hotel in 1980. Very modern rooms, small swimming pool. From 186 € (235 € during congresses).

LUXURY HOTELS

If you can't afford spending the night, treat yourself to breakfast (from 16 to 25 €).

Hotel Claris (**B** D1)
→ *Carrer de Pau Claris, 150*
Tel. 93 487 62 62
A 19th-century palace converted into a modern and very beautiful hotel using a mixture of exotic wood, metal, marble and 4th-century mosaics in its decoration. From 330 €.

Hotel Ritz (**B** CD2)
→ *Gran Vía de les Corts Catalanes, 668*
Tel. 93 318 52 00
The most elegant and luxurious of Barcelona's historic hotels, opened in 1919. From 337 €.

Hotel Arts (**F** B5)
→ *Carrer de la Marina, 19*
Tel. 93 221 10 00
www.harts.es
Avant-garde architecture and luxury over 44 floors, facing the sea. From 355 €.

Centre principal TMB
→ **M** *Universitat*
Tel. 93 318 70 74
Mon-Fri 8am–8pm
Information
→ *Tel. 010*
Subway
→ *Sun-Thu and public hols 5am–midnight; Fri-Sat and eves of public hols 5am–2am; Five lines, trains every 5 mins (8 mins w/e).*
Bus
→ *Daily 6am–10.30pm, every 10-15 mins* Night bus: 16 lines, 10.30pm–4.30am, every 20-30 mins.
Tickets (metro/bus)
From ticket offices and ticket machines.
Single ticket
→ *1.05 €*
Carta T-DIA
→ *1-day pass (4.40 €)*
Carta T-10
→ *10 journeys (5.80 €)*
Prices
→ *3 days: 11.30 €*
→ *5 days: 17.30 €*

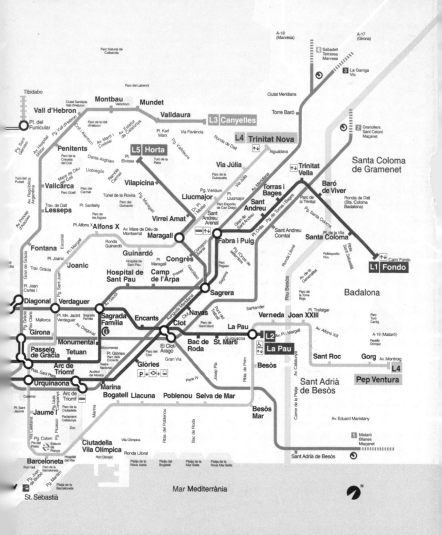

Horaris / Horarios / Timetable			
5:00 - 23:00 h	Feiners (excepte divendres i vigílies de	Laborables (ex. viernes y víspera de festivo)	Weekday (except Friday and day before bank holiday)
5:00 - 2:00 h	Divendres, dissabtes i vigílies de festiu	Viernes, sábados y vísperas de festivos	Friday, Saturday and day before bank holiday
6:00 - 23:00 h	Festius entre setmana	Festivos entre semana	Bank holiday
6:00 - 2:00 h	Festius vigília d'un altre festiu	Festivos víspera de otro festivo	Day before bank holiday
6:00 - 24:00 h	Diumenge	Domingos	Sunday